Peggy Harris

Life on a
Dartmoor Scrapyard

Peggy Harris

LIFE ON A DARTMOOR SCRAPYARD

FOREWORD BY CHRIS CHAPMAN

EDGEMOOR
PUBLISHING

For my daughter Clare, for my brothers Jim and Bob, and my Mother and Father.

First published 2009. Reprinted 2011
Published by Edgemoor Publishing Limited
Wykeham House, Station Road, Okehampton, Devon EX20 1DY

© Peggy Harris 2009

Some of the stories published in this book have appeared in *Dartmoor Magazine*
www.dartmoormagazine.co.uk

Edited by Sue Viccars
Designed by Simon Lloyd

British Library Cataloguing in Publication Data.
A catalogue record for this book is available from the British Library.

ISBN 978-0-9564246-0-0

Typesetting and origination by Edgemoor Publishing Limited.
Printed in Great Britain by Short Run Press Ltd.

Front cover Sam Harris, scrapman, Lettaford, 1986 © *Chris Chapman*
Page 2 Peggy and Donkey Jack *Courtesy of Peggy Harris*
Page 128 Sam Harris, 1977 *Courtesy of Peggy Harris*
Back cover Peter and Fred Hutchings with Sam Harris, Yardworthy Pony Drift,
1981 © *Chris Chapman*

CONTENTS

FOREWORD

In order to explain how I came to know Peggy and her famous father Sam, I first have to tell you a little of my driving history. When I moved to Dartmoor in the mid 1970s my mode of transport was a Reliant Regal three-wheeler van.

I gained a motorcycle licence at the age of 18, and because of an odd loophole in the law the licence enabled one to 'ride' a tricycle. Bond made three-wheelers with a Villiers motorcycle engine mounted over the front wheel, complete with kick-start. It was in all respects a car, but having no reverse gear the Department of Transport classed it as a tricycle. After dabbling with motorbikes I decided to buy one of these, a Mark G, although the advantage of being dry was soon outweighed by its numerous failings. Far too often I would stall at a set of traffic lights just as they were turning green, and then suffer the embarrassment of having to clamber out, lift the bonnet and kick the engine back into life. By the time I was back in the driving seat the lights would be on red, including the tempers of a number of motorists stuck in the queue behind me.

However I then discovered that Reliant produced a three-wheeler with cabin ignition and a gearbox complete with reverse gear, although for some strange reason it too was classed as a tricycle. So, ..I could now drive a proper motor car, and without a full licence!

In those early days on Dartmoor I had very little money and keeping this fibreglass contraption on the road was something of a nightmare. Then one day I was introduced to David Leaman in Chagford. He owned an earlier version of the vehicle and, as he worked out at Lettaford, had in his garden shed a large collection of Reliant bits gleaned from Sam's scrapyard. Through Dave I kept mine going for about three years but then, at the age of 28, I decided to take my driving test. I passed first time and moved up to the luxury of a Morris 1000 van.

These were great cars and very easy to work on, and needless to say I soon discovered that Sam's scrapyard at Lettaford was a gold mine for spare parts. Sam's friendly nature, coupled with 'that'll be 50p', gained him a constant flow of trade from me and many of my friends.

Sam Harris, 1981 *James Tilly*

I remember the children being around in the background, not quite as oily looking as Sam, but they were such a part of the scene that at first I didn't pay too much attention to them. Then one day I spotted Jim Harris and some friends trying to push start a homemade go-kart on the road above Tunnaford Farm. I photographed them and over the next few years added pictures of Sam, Bob and his twin sister Peggy riding her 'Donkey Jack' at the Yardworthy Pony Drift to my archive. Jim, Peggy's older brother, introduced me to his pet tawny owl at the scrapyard which he called Ollie. It's one of my favourite pictures.

After Sam died I didn't see Peggy again for a good many years until one day I was up at Frenchbeer Farm photographing the Christmas turkey plucking. Peggy was working in the shed with her friend Roy and reintroduced herself. She was a little shy at first, but some months later brought me a selection of her written stories and asked if I would read them. I sat down that very night and was hooked. Peggy has a natural talent for telling a story. I thought them absolutely wonderful.

It is true that Peggy and her siblings had a hard life, and no doubt at times found mixing with others of their age difficult because of where and how they lived. But in our increasingly homogenised countryside, one can't help but feel a little envy. Her stories tell of a Dartmoor that quietly existed without too much interference, their lives were rich in lots of ways, and were the family still in business today no doubt they would be hailed as local heroes – The Green Gleaners, The Lettaford Recyclers, bring us your carbon footprints and we'll squelch them in the mud. If, like me, you love Dartmoor, and love a peopled landscape as well as one of wild beauty, you will thoroughly enjoy Peggy's recollections in this book. They certainly make me smile.

Chris Chapman
Throwleigh, Dartmoor
October 2009

INTRODUCTION

ABOUT ME

I wonder if you remember us, the kids running wild in the scrapyard? I think people regarded us as tougher than their kids and used to the hardships of our lives, or somehow bred to it, but in reality we were just ordinary kids. We looked different – brown as berries in the summertime from the wind and sun, and I must admit pretty grubby sometimes, but then we were working as hard as most men from an early age.

I was born Margaret Harris in 1966, but everyone calls me Peggy. My brother Bob and I were twins and I have an older brother called Jim, born in 1964. We were all raised in a scrapyard on the edge of Dartmoor, three miles from Chagford, the nearest village, and where I eventually went to primary school.

My father Sam started the scrapyard in the late forties, early fifties. He was picking up mixed loads of scrap and needed somewhere to sort and save it, so he rented three acres of land from Chris Hill, a farmer in Lettaford. Gradually over the years he bought this land and made his home there.

Peggy (aged about six), Bob and Jim
Courtesy of Peggy Harris

At first Father lived in an old gypsy caravan on the site, and then in a succession of more modern secondhand static caravans. Later he bought an old wooden chalet and we lived in that, but we still used the caravans too.

My mother was born in Southampton and moved down to a Dartmoor farm a couple of miles away from the scrapyard with her family. She worked in Bristol for several years, lodging in a hostel. She met up with my father and they married in 1963. Jim was born the following year, and they brought up the whole family on the scrapyard.

When we were little, I remember, my twin and I were locked up in a caravan for hours each day and didn't run about outside until we were nearly three. A scrapyard is a dangerous place for small children and my Mother was working with my Father outside with no time to watch us.

My eldest brother Jim was the apple of my Dad's eye, but it was different for me and my twin brother. My Mother was fond of Bob but I was the mistake, the runt of the family – and, worst of all, I was a girl! They wanted all boys, so they brought me up like a boy and expected me to work like one. When we were big enough we were expected to help load the lorry. My Mother's most famous words were 'All hands on deck!'

My brothers and I had everything kids could dream of – and on the other hand we had nothing. Nothing belongs to you on a scrapyard. You only get to keep something until somebody comes and wants to buy it. We could make up push bikes from spare parts, make go-carts, play hide-and-seek in the old cars, we could drive cars, ride motorbikes – but when you came home from school whatever we had made could be gone. Father would have sold it or given it away. This would make us angry, but it happened time and time again. Our games were more dangerous and exciting than most children's games though, and this made up for not having toys or not getting to keep the things we found or made.

Living near the edge of the moor is really exposed to the elements, but it's even more extreme when you live in a caravan all year round. In the summer when it's hot it's even hotter in a scrapyard. The sun's rays bounce off the car windows and are reflected from hot shiny metal and the car bodies act like radiators. It made it very hot to work in the yard too, and handling the scrap could get quite dangerous. The black tyres would get almost too hot to handle, and you could burn your hands touching the scrap iron. In the hot summer of 1976 I burnt the backs of my legs by sitting on a car tyre.

We were living in a caravan in that year and it was like sleeping in an oven at night, it was so stuffy. At night, as the heat of the day faded away, you could hear the popping of metal drums and the creaking of the cars as they cooled and settled. It was a regular thing to be in the bath in the open air in summertime. Mother kept it up until we were 10 and Jim was 12! She would have three tin baths with round handles on each end and she would park us in a row on the back of this old furniture lorry with its tailboard down like a platform. The customers would all make remarks on how white we were turning, when earlier we would have been as black as crows. These baths were about a foot deep and we would try to hide and screw up into a ball out of sight. We were so embarrassed. We hated Sundays.

When it rained the yard got very muddy as it was not surfaced, but was still just a field under all the scrap. With all the oil which had spilled and seeped from scrap cars over the years we would be working in black oily mud. The tractor and lorries going in and out would make deep ruts filled with oily muddy water and we lived in our welly boots. It made work doubly hard slogging through the mud, which would sometimes be over the tops of our boots. Keeping clean was made even more difficult as we had no mains or piped water. We used rainwater, collected in big tanks around the yard, to wash in, and Mother used it to wash clothes too.

Wintertime at the scrapyard could be very severe. Up near the moor the temperature can plummet in a very short space of time. When it froze you couldn't pick up iron because it would be stuck fast in the icy ground and your hands would stick to it too. We couldn't operate machinery, as it too would be stuck to the ground by its wheels or tracks. If it snowed you couldn't even find the scrap to load: the cars would be carpeted with a layer of thick snow. When we walked through the yard you could hear your feet crunching through the snow until you came to a puddle. You would hear a crunch, then a crack under your boot just before it disappeared into the black oily mud beneath, which would then ooze up over the white snow, leaving strange black footprints behind us.

Although Father was held up by the weather, we kids were always delighted as it meant we stayed home from school. Being one of the most isolated homes in the area we were usually the first cut off by the snowdrifts and the last to thaw out. We would go up to Lettaford with plastic sacks and slide down a steep field with other kids from the hamlet, or roll snowballs down the hill to see how big we could make them.

We had no mains electricity either, so Mother used to boil up the copper for hot water and used a mangle to wring things out. She was quite inventive and made an airing cupboard out of an old metal cupboard with paraffin heaters in the bottom and hung the clothes in there to dry. When the weather was bad she found it hard to dry clothes and sometimes in winter I went to school in damp things, as they hadn't dried. The other kids must have wondered at the steam rising from us on the bus.

Drinking water was fetched in two buckets every day, or every other day, and carried from the river about 600 yards away. Mother and us kids fetched water, but I never saw Father fetch any. Mother found a good water pump in the scrap once, which she wanted Father to fix up to bring water piped from the river, but he sold it before she could get him to do it for her.

We used to hang the water buckets out by the back door and as soon as you picked up the buckets and they knocked together the dogs always appeared, and – together with the cat – would accompany you to the river and back.

In a scrapyard everything you need has been recycled from something else, and most of our requirements were satisfied in this way. Mother would usually choose our clothes from the jumble sale leftovers, which we would pick up most Saturdays from villages round about. There was nearly always a jumble sale somewhere, either Chagford, Moretonhampstead, Lustleigh or Widecombe. When it came to our school clothes Mother sometimes had to buy them but she only bought for the biggest and then they got handed down, as money was always tight. I was the smallest, so they were well worn by the time they reached me.

When we came home from school we had to change out of our school clothes. We couldn't risk getting them dirty. Mother wouldn't let us out in the yard in them as she only washed once a week and we only had one set of school things each.

Mother had her own inventive forms of discipline. If we had done something wrong, she would ground us by taking away our play clothes and would take our school clothes off us as well. All that was left to wear were our bed things so we had to go to bed!

As I got older my parents always made me feel I wasn't good enough, so I would try and prove that I was as strong as any of the boys. I would lift a car engine out of the back of the lorry and see how far I could carry it, or lift a car by its wings and take off the wheels with no jack. Maybe I couldn't compete in working like a boy but my real strength lay elsewhere.

When I was nine I found a way to get away: I met the Ardens. I first met Clare; she was three years younger than me but fun. She had a pony and I was invited over for a ride. I was hooked!

They taught me to ride so I could now ride Donkey Jack better. I learned to control him better from the skills I learned with the Ardens. I started going over every weekend and I didn't mind if I had to shift dung all day. It was away from home and I was doing something I enjoyed and getting good at it. The Ardens made their living breaking in horses and ponies, and I helped bring the young ponies on until they were sold or sent back to their owners. They also did riding treks and driving lessons. I spent a lot of time riding young ponies 'shot gun'. This meant I rode at the back of the group and kept all the holidaymakers who had never ridden up together. I would give them hints about how to ride and shout 'Stop!' when someone fell off, which happened quite often.

I left the scrapyard in September 1986 and went to Hittisleigh to have my daughter, Clare. I went back and worked there until 1988, when I left for good to raise Clare in Exeter. My Father died in November that year after a short illness, and my brother Bob ran the scrapyard for a short while after that.

The days of allowing a scrapyard to flourish in a National Park are long gone, and new legislation enforced by the local authorities meant the yard was forced to close and an expensive clean up of the land was expected, causing endless worry for Bob. My recollections are of mixed happiness and misery there but one thing is certain: they are unique memories, which I hope you will enjoy sharing.

My Father Sam

'Good old Sam' – that's what everybody said. He was a well-loved and well-known man, short and stocky, a true local character: I remember he wore bib-brace overalls and a neckerchief, a flat cap and wellies – and (before he gave up smoking) always had a fag hanging out of his mouth. I felt he put his customers first, and could have done more for his family; simple things like providing us with a proper home. Although he brought a smile to people's faces, behind closed doors things weren't always rosy. Us kids had a sort of love-hate relationship with him.

Sam Harris was born in 1915, and came over to Dartmoor from Iddesleigh, in mid Devon, in 1936. He went to work on the dam for Fernworthy reservoir. His first job was to break stone with a sledgehammer, but then he used stone crushers. At this time he lived at Lingcombe Farm, Chagford, in a hut up in a field. He used to say he 'could see the searchlights from Plymouth' during the war. He reckoned when the planes flew over very low his hut would rattle and shake. He said they came so low he could see the pilot.

Then he moved over to Long Lane. He lived in several places there, on farms, usually in a caravan. He later rented land down at West Combe and milked cows. He also had a few sheep and bought and sold horses and ponies. People often said that they had seen Sam with a string of horses and ponies tied nose to tail, walking to sales. He worked for farmers, shearing and haymaking. During this time he also had to be in the Home Guard. He would have to walk to Moretonhampstead, four miles away, to perform guard duties every evening. He would have to make roadblocks that were to stop tanks, repel mock attacks and guard the churchyard. All he had to defend himself with was a broomstick handle.

One night he was on guard duty in the churchyard, armed with his broomstick handle. It rained heavily all night. In the morning the colonel turned up on his horse. He asked Sam, in his snooty voice, 'Did you see anything?' 'No,' replied Sam grumpily, 'the sky opened all night and the rain's running out of me arse! And who in their right mind would want to come in 'ere? And them in 'ere, sure as 'ell ain't no one is coming out!' When he finished his guard duty he would have to walk home to milk the cows and do a whole day's work. He stuck at this for a while, and then found out that as he lived over three miles away he didn't have to do it any more.

American soldiers were based up on Mardon, just above Moretonhampstead. Sam would often have deals with the soldiers: he would get big cans of corned beef, fags and overalls. He said he would have to button up his coat whenever he saw American officers as his overalls had USA stamped across the chest. Sam said when the Americans moved out for D-Day the trucks and troop carriers were bumper to bumper right out over the moor leading to Plymouth. He said you could hardly cross the main road.

By then the horse trade was coming to an end; people didn't want horses and ponies so much. Farmers were buying tractors, people were buying cars. Sam could see that horse equipment like ploughs was going to go to waste, so he started to buy up the scrap. He would collect it all up in heaps all in different places. When he had enough he would drag it down to Moretonhampstead station, to load railway trucks. It took many days by horse and cart at first. He then learnt to drive and delivered the non-ferrous metals to E. Pearse Ltd in Newton Abbot.

At this time Sam rented a bit of rough ground at Lettaford from Chris Hill, and eventually bought it: it became known as Sam's Scrapyard. At first he lived in an old lean-to shed and shared it with his horse. He would fry his breakfast on a small fire in the morning. He often said that he would have to be quick when cooking as when he wasn't looking the horse would lean over and pinch his bacon straight from the pan. Through one of his deals he later came across a showman's van and lived in that, then moved onto various caravans. He was never bothered about home comforts: as long as he had enough food to eat and enough money in his pocket to have a deal, he was happy. He often said that he never wanted to be the richest man in the churchyard.

Angel, Cherry, Myrtle and Doreen at Lingcombe in the 1940s
Courtesy of Peggy Harris

My Mother

I remember her always wearing jeans, wellies and a flat cap. She was a hard woman, with no love in her for us kids; well, we never saw any. She was 40 when I was born, so I have watched her go grey and grow old. She worked hard to raise us and cook the meals and look after the yard when Father was out. As we grew up she worked, driving the lorry, picking up scrap and delivering sorted metals to Exeter or Newton Abbot.

I know she did her best in difficult circumstances. She suffered from paranoia and always had a bogeyman after her when we were young. She always thought someone was watching or spying on her. Father was unsympathetic and would wind her up; then us kids would get it.

My mother was born Doreen Baker in 1926 in Park Gate near Southampton. She was one of seven. Her father was a carpenter and then became a farmer; her mother was a seamstress. Her mother had also lost three children. Doreen's Aunt Hilda had also lost a child and couldn't have any more, so she asked if she could take one of the children out for the day, on holidays and weekends. Doreen was the fourth eldest. Aunt Hilda didn't want to take Myrtle, the eldest, as she was a plain-looking girl and was more help to her mother. Rodney was a weak boy and Cherry wasn't a cuddly child, but Doreen was a pretty three-year-old.

Aunt Hilda lived not far away, just down the lane. Doreen's mother couldn't see any harm in her going with Aunt Hilda as she had half a dozen children already.

Aunt Hilda would pick Doreen up and take her home and put her in new dresses and treat her as her own child. On returning Doreen she would change her back in her old clothes and send her home, with a bag of sweets and biscuits, telling her that they were all for her. Doreen's mother had brought her children up to share, so her elder sister Cherry would take the bag from her, taking a sweet and then handing the bag back, telling her to share them.

The Second World War broke out when Doreen was 13. She often spoke about living in a black out, and having to sit in the air raid shelter, listening to the planes that would fly over, and the doodlebug bombs dropping. Her school was bombed when she was 14, so she never went back. Her Aunt also died about this time so she had to stay home with her family. During the war her father kept cows and hens, and sold the milk and the eggs. She had to stay home and help.

When she was 19 her family moved to Devon. They bought a farm just outside Chagford, called Lingcombe. The family didn't have much money, so they had to plant potatoes, and she stayed home for two years before getting a job in Chagford. She then got a job in Woolworths in Exeter; she would have to walk three miles to Chagford to catch a bus. Later she stayed in a hostel in Grendon Road and went home at weekends.

She then moved to work in a cardboard factory in Bristol, and later a milk bottle factory. She would go home some weekends, on her BSA Bantam motorbike. Her sister told me many a time she would come home happy, and something would upset her; she would be slamming doors and storming off back to Bristol. She was nicknamed the 'wicked witch from the east'.

Before she came back to Devon for good she had seen a clairvoyant who told her she was going to have three boys. She moved back to Devon in her mid thirties. She was feeling left on the shelf: she wasn't married. She went to visit Sam Harris, a local scrap dealer, who she'd known before she moved to Bristol. They say she went over and 'hung up her hat'. She would go across the fields to Sam's and do the housework, tidying up his caravan. There was a Scotsman, Jock, who worked for Sam; he was more times drunk than he was sober. He was joking around one day and asked Doreen to marry him, but she turned him down flat. So Sam asked her to marry him and she said yes. They were married at Newton Abbot Registry office in 1963.

The following year she gave birth to a boy and called him James William, but he was known as Jim. She was a doting mother, fully convinced that Jim was talking to her and she could understand all his googlings and wooglings. Then on 12th October 1966 she gave birth to twins, a boy and a girl. She was a bit surprised as she thought she was going to have two more boys. She called the boy Robert George and the girl, me, Margaret Elizabeth, but we were known as Bob and Peggy. I don't know if she was pleased or not to have a girl, but she often told me I wan't a cuddly baby; I would turn away from her, and if she went to cuddle me I would put my arm in the way. She said she never bothered since.

HOW I STARTED TO WRITE

When I left school I could hardly read and write. If I had to fill in forms I couldn't spell my full name. When I read to my daughter Clare I found it hard to read simple stories, and I would skip the words I didn't know and make up something else. Later I found that when I went shopping I would buy something because of the picture on the tin, and then at home find it was something I didn't want.

I met a lady called Margaret New who used to be a special needs teacher. She offered to help me with reading and writing, which she did for several months, and I improved a little. She also helped my daughter to read. Clare was behind on her reading and writing and I felt it was more important for her to catch up, so I just muddled along.

Then in 2003 I went through a very stressful time. I suffered from depression and couldn't work due to a bad back. I had to sign on at the Job Centre, and told the lady there about my problems with reading and writing. She told me of a course that I could go on for six months to help, after which I would feel better and be able to look for a new job.

The course was at the Westward Training Centre, Exeter. I remember it well. There were five adults sat around a cluster of tables. I remember thinking, 'How am I going to cope with this lot?' One was an ex-biker, covered in tattoos with yellow skin from his alcohol problem. Next one to him was a very big man, like a bouncer, and then there was a little lady covered in cat hairs. She was a cat lover and just talked about her babies, meaning cats. Then there was young man who had that 'piss off' attitude, always ready for a fight. Sat next to me was a very smartly dressed lady with very small eyes. What really stood out from looking at them was that four of them had no front teeth at all.

Jane Russell was our tutor. She would set us each different pieces of work, as we were all at different levels. One morning she told us that she wanted us all to write a short story. We were supposed to make one up. I said I couldn't make one up, but that I could tell her a story all the same. So I sat back in my chair and started to tell the class about my childhood, growing up with Donkey Jack. They couldn't believe the stories were true.

Jane leaned over my shoulder and asked me to write what I had just told the group. So I wrote down the story about when Donkey Jack met the hounds. Jane showed her colleagues my story and they all said that I should write more. So I wrote several more, and then it was suggested that I should publish them. I thought they were just saying that to make me feel good. But time went by and I met Chris Chapman, who used to take pictures of us and Father at the scrapyard when we were young. He read my stories, and passed them on to a friend's wife, who was the then editor of *Dartmoor Magazine*, and that's how it all got started.

Peggy at G. H. Newbery & Son Ltd, scrap merchants, Exeter
Courtesy of Peggy Harris

ALL ABOUT SAM

LIVING WITH MY FATHER

Father was a very easy-going man, a happy-go-lucky sort of
bloke. Well known for his cheap deals and generosity. Customers
thought he was wonderful; even 20 years on people think fondly
of him. He would pick up their old cars and scrap and give them
something for it, and when they wanted something for their
cars or a piece of metal they would come to see Sam as he was
always cheap. 'Good old Sam' you would hear people say, 'what
a wonderful place, you can find anything.' He rarely told us kids
off. You would hear him say to Mother, 'They kids, sort them out.'
Mother would say that Father loaded the gun and she fired it, and
we would get a double barrel.

If we knew Father was off out in the lorry we would often ask
if we could go with him. He rarely said 'No' so we would hang
around up the lane near the lorry, waiting for him. If he seemed
to have disappeared we would go and find him and ask him if he
was still going. 'Dreckly' he would reply, meaning 'In a minute'.
So my brothers and I would go back up the lane and wait, but if
you went off for a drink or to get something you would hear the
lorry start up and Father was off. He wouldn't shout for you, he
would drive off slowly up the lane. Many a time I ran after him
shouting for him to stop. But he never stopped. We would nearly
catch up. Tired from the running and shouting I would fall in the
dusty lane, heartbroken, and Father would just drive on. I think
he used to wait for us to disappear so he would go without us, but
as we got bigger we could run faster and jump on and up over the
tailboard and bang on the window for him to stop.

Mother and I came home one evening after a busy day picking
up scrap. We met two old farmers walking up the lane rolling a
lorry wheel. I looked close; it was only the spare wheel for our
lorry, and I'd just had a puncture fixed on it that had cost us £10.
I said to the two old boys: 'I'm sorry you can't have that, that's our
spare tyre.' 'We've just bought it off Sam,' they replied. I could
see Father stood at the entrance of the scrapyard and I shouted
over to him, 'You can't sell that tyre to them, it's our spare one!'
'I have!' He replied. I thought he'd let them have it for a fiver
so I offered them a fiver, and said I was sorry but they couldn't

Sam in James Douglas's cottage, Spreyton *James Tilly*

have that wheel. I shouted to Mother to back me up, but she just walked away.

Father told these two old men, 'Don't worry, I should have had her locked up years ago in Digby.' He implied I was mad, so these two old men loaded up the wheel and went. I lost it and probably did look a bit mad! I went in and counted the till, and counted it again after Father had put the money in from the sale of the wheel. He'd only sold it for a pound. I was furious with him. It was as if Father would always put a spanner in the works so we couldn't get on.

FATHER SAW RED

People came from miles away to buy parts from the scrapyard. There was a time I remember when us kids was young. Two young men came to the yard with a small child; they wanted some parts of an Austin. Father said there was one down by the beech trees.

'Go out in the yard and turn down right, don't touch the first Austin, as the engine has been sold. There's another down near the baler.' We were having dinner and the two men were going in and out of the yard up the lane to their car and back, fetching tools. Eventually they came to the door to pay for the parts that they had.

Father was suspicious, so he went down to the Austin to check the engine he had sold. He found the carburettor was missing. I remember him marching up the lane to where the men were parked. They were putting their tools in the boot of their car. Father went up to them, and said, 'I told you not to touch that Austin engine.' The two men insisted that they hadn't touched it. Father told them that he was going to search their car. He looked through the boot and then inside the car.

Under the seat he found the carburettor. He held it up and asked which one had taken it. They still insisted that they hadn't taken it, and said that the toddler must have put hidden it. Father said, 'You're telling me that dear little boy took it off and put it under the seat?' Father was livid that they were accusing the toddler, and told Mother to call the police. I think this was the first time ever that I heard Father disgusted with anyone.

THE DAY THAT SAM GOT LOCKED UP

All sorts of people would come and sell all sorts of scrap to us. One day a chap and his brother arrived with some old household wire and asked if they could burn it as it was worth more burnt than with the plastic on. Sam said that was OK. Later on that evening a police car and van arrived full of police officers. They asked if a certain couple of blokes had been up and had he (Sam) bought any hot stuff from them. Sam said, 'Yes, it was rather hot' and with that the officer arrested him. They took him off for the night and put him in a cell.

Sometime later he had to go to court to stand before the judge. He was asked again if he had handled hot goods because he'd said he had to the arresting officer. Sam said the wire was so hot it had burnt his hands and melted the bag; he was talking about the bag of burnt wire that he had bought! He didn't know if it was stolen because he never asked. The judge chucked the case out.

OLD COAT

Arthur Raymont, who used to farm at Vogwell, told me a tale about how he found a coat of Sam's in one of his fields. Sam had been sorting his ponies and had taken his coat off and left it up in the hedge. It stayed there for some time, several weeks. One day he arrived in Arthur's yard and asked if he'd seen his coat – was it still in the field?

'Oh yeah,' replied Arthur, so they went to fetch it. 'It be rotten by now,' said Arthur. Sam picked it and put his hand in one of its pockets and pulled out a big bundle of money. 'Cor,' said Arthur, 'you was lucky that no one picked it up!' Sam replied, 'Who would want an old coat like this!'

FOGGY ROAD

Arthur and Sam went to the Goosey Fair in Tavistock one October. They had to go over the moor to get home. They had left late; it was really foggy by then. They both had to look out of their windows to see where they were going, by following the edge of the road. The fog was so thick that they could hardly see the road. They crawled along, and then seemed to go through a large gateway. They found that they had driven into a large yard, with big tall dark walls. So they got out, and found that they had driven into the Dartmoor prison yard. Sam said 'Bugger boy, we don't wanna stay in here!'

SHOT AT A RAT

Sam was down Hennock picking up scrap from Ian Burgoyne. They were having a cup of tea before loading the scrap, when they noticed a young policeman snooping around the farmyard. He was nosing into things without permission.

Ian fetched his gun, and when the policeman got close to the dung heap he let fire at him. The policeman took off. It wasn't long before the sergeant arrived and said, 'What was the idea you shooting at my constable?'

'What constable?' Ian replied. 'I was shooting at a rat on the dung heap.'

STUCK IN THE MUD

Sam went out to South Tawton to pick up some scrap from Ian, who'd moved there from Hennock and lived down in the woods with his family. There were two tracks leading through the woods to get to his place. It had been raining; there was very clayey soil out that way. The track lead down between the trees over the tree roots. There were big potholes filled up with murky water and very sticky mud.

Sam and the workman left the truck at the end of track and started walking along it. Sam splashed through the puddles and waded through the sticky mud. The workman picked his way up and around the edge. All of a sudden Sam was up to his waist. He had stepped into a puddle, fallen over and sunk. He couldn't get out, and the workman couldn't pull him out, so Sam told him to go and fetch Ian to help.

The workman and Ian returned with a mule. Ian tied a rope around Sam and hitched him to the mule. They say the mule grunted, brayed and farted as he pulled Sam out.

WAVING ON A CAR THAT WASN'T THERE

One of Father's favourite pubs was the Warren House Inn. It sits alone on the edge of the main road that runs across Dartmoor, surrounded by miles of open wilderness, mounds of purple heather and clumps of gorse, with dips and mine workings as far as the eye can see.

One night my Father went out drinking there with a close friend, Roy Mortimore. Come closing time they staggered out of the warm, smoky pub into the crisp night air, where a blanket of frost tinted the moorland. It sparkled in the moonlight. A group of sheep huddled along the roadside under the windowsill. They moved slightly as Father staggered towards his car.

People got away with drink driving back in the sixties. There weren't many policemen around the moor back then.

It was a lovely moonlit night. They bundled into Father's black Austin and headed home. On the way, Father was dazzled by a bright light in the interior mirror and in the little round wing mirrors. The light was so bright he couldn't see. He wound down his window and tried to wave the car on but no one passed. The light was still very bright so he tried again but still no one passed.

Eventually he pulled over and stopped to let the car go by but still it didn't pass. He asked Roy if he could see anyone, just checking it wasn't his drunkenness. Roy slurred, 'Yeah, he's still there!' So my Father got out of the car and staggered to the back to see who was there. When he looked there was no one there, just the moon beaming down at him. He had been waving on the moon!

PICTURE ON THE WALL

Back in the late fifties Father was out with his friend Mark Small drinking up at the Warren House Inn. They'd been there all afternoon. The Warren House Inn is the highest pub on Dartmoor. There are always lots of tourists visiting the moor from all around the world.

This day a group of Americans called in. They were talking to the locals, asking questions about the pub and the moor when they noticed a picture of a naked man strapped to a Dartmoor pony on the wall. When they asked what it was about my Father told them, 'It was when married men went astray. The women would tie them to a wild stallion and let it go.' The Americans were shocked by this and asked if it still happened. 'Oh no,' said Father, 'they ran out of stallions!'

BROKEN RIBS

Father was out at Sticklepath picking up scrap from two Indians who couldn't speak very good English.

Father needed the toilet but he didn't like to ask the customers. For one thing he had muddy boots with scrapyard dirt on them, and he was afraid he might leave black oily footprints on the carpet, and secondly he had trouble taking his boots off. We always had to help him put them on in the morning. So on the way home he decided to climb over the hedge, as he was getting desperate. He hadn't noticed that there was a six-foot drop on the other side until it was too late. He fell and landed on a rock and broke three ribs. He had knocked himself out in the fall, and when he came round he had to pull himself back up over the hedge and then drive home a good 20 miles through the country lanes in an old lorry with no power steering.

At the time he was a heavy smoker, and regularly smoked 60 Woodbines a day. With his broken ribs and the heavy steering it made him cough. Every time he coughed he nearly blacked out. It took him hours to get home and several weeks to get over it and to cap it all he couldn't use the toilet for ten days!

BLACKINGSTONE QUARRY

Father went and bought some scrap from Blackingstone Quarry. One of his buys was the old weighbridge. Father would use a 14lb sledgehammer, or cut things up with gas. The bridge was too big and thick for him to smack up with his sledge, and he couldn't use gas as it doesn't cut well.

Father knew a man called Lionel Wadman in Throwleigh who used to be an explosive expert when he was in the army. They had no problem getting explosive at the quarry. Lionel laid the explosive; they all took cover. Father said, 'There was an almighty bang! The weighbridge went up in the air whole and came down like rain.' He spent a few hours collecting bits of the weighbridge in his tin bucket.

LOST THE CAR

One day in the early sixties Father was on his way home from over the moor. He'd turned to go down to Jurston. As he went down the hill past the old gravel pit he saw a man in the road. It was Tom Fitzpatrick, the local taxi driver from Chagford. Father pulled up and asked him what he was doing up here. Old Tom Fitzpatrick said he had pulled up for a pee, and was admiring the view, but when he turned round the car was gone.

Father said he hadn't passed a car further up the road, so old Fitzpatrick jumped in with him. They headed down over the hill; there was no sign of the car. They were looking for a big old Morris, the one with big round headlamps. The car had rolled away as the hand brake hadn't held. The car ran down the road, and when it ran into the hedge its big spring bumper bounced it back and it rolled on round a sharp corner and down a very steep hill to Jurston. It was very lucky; there wasn't many cars around in those days and they eventually found the car on the bottom green at Jurston. It must have travelled a good mile, yet there wasn't a scratch on it.

An aerial view of Sam's scrapyard, said by some to resemble either a box of Liquorice Allsorts or a show field! *Courtesy of Peggy Harris*

MORETONHAMPSTEAD TO LUSTLEIGH LINE

After Beeching closed the railways, the Moretonhampstead to Lustleigh line was bought and sold several times. Eventually the rails themselves were gone, leaving only the chairs (the lumps of iron that hold the rails in place). Father bought all the chairs from Moreton to Lustleigh. He worked out what each chair weighed: eight chairs to a hundredweight, 20 hundredweight to a ton. For several years he had used the railway to dray his scrap away, and now he drayed a part of the railway by road.

OUTSIDE THE POLICE STATION

Father was always towing cars home; he rarely looked in his mirrors to see if the car he was towing was still there. Over the years he had several people working for him, and I bet if you spoke to them now and asked them if they got home in one piece without losing a wheel, or coming unhitched, they would tell you a tale.

On one of his journeys he went to pick up a car from Okehampton Camp. I don't remember the name of the workman, but Father hitched the car up to his lorry with a rope and set off. Father always drove the back roads. On arriving home he got out of his cab and shouted to the workman, 'Wanna cup of tea?' When there was no answer Father walked to the back of the lorry – and there was no car and no workman. So Father started up and went looking for them. Going back through the narrow lanes all the way back to Okehampton he eventually found the car and the workman right outside the police station, on George Street, with a policeman.

The policeman had come out of the station and found a non-roadworthy car stopped in the road. He'd gone over and looked in the window and noticed that there wasn't any road tax. Then he looked around the car and could see a couple of bald tyres. The policeman asked the workman what he was doing driving a non-roadworthy car with no tax in Okehampton. The workman explained that he was being towed by Sam Harris, the local scrap dealer, the rope had broken and Sam had gone on without him.

The policeman didn't believe him and was going to book him as he believed the workman was driving the vehicle. 'How could I be driving it? It's got no engine!' he said, lifting the bonnet and showing him. By now he was getting worked up as he was afraid he was going to be booked, but just in time Father appeared and settled the matter before towing him home.

Sam's Pick-up

Father often bought pick-ups or vans with nine to twelve months' MOT. The scrap trade would take its toll on any vehicle, and in the last couple of months the vehicles would start looking rough. Father was pulled in one evening by a police officer. He told Father that his vehicle wasn't fit to be on the road and he shouldn't be driving it. So Father took out the keys and gave them to the officer and started walking off, saying, 'Well you can have it then!' The poor officer was stunned.

Father bought a diesel pick-up from a man called Soby. It had 12 months' MOT but it smoked a bit. Most deals went on in the evening, out in the dark and you didn't know what you really had until the morning. Soby did say it smoked, but didn't say how much. Father was in Moretonhampstead when a local policeman was directing traffic. Sam was waiting to go, but said he couldn't see the policeman in the mirror for black smoke. He said he heard the policeman shout, 'Move it Sam! I can't see.' He was surrounded in black smoke, coughing and choking.

Sam was Heard to Say

Sam had an old Austin A40 that came in for scrap. The car wasn't worth much, but he knew someone who wanted the boot lid and that was worth more than the car. He had a chap working for him nicknamed Weasel. When Weasel was pushing the cars in with the Chaseside tractor Sam told him not to damage the Austin A40 boot lid as he had sold it. Weasel acknowledged this. With a crash and a bang he smashed it right up the arse and ruined the back end of the A40. Sam was livid! He went up to Weasel and said, 'You silly bugger! Your mother should have smacked you over the head when you was born and fed a suck pig on the milk – that would have bin more useful!'

PEOPLE WHO PINCH

One cold, windy day a customer had come to look around the
yard. Father was outside, and met the customer coming out.
He said he couldn't find anything, and stood chatting to Sam.
The customer had picked up a fan belt while he was in the yard,
had rolled it up and put it in his pocket. While chatting the fan
belt unrolled itself, flicked out of his pocket and landed on the
ground. The customer took no notice and carried on chatting.
Sam noticed the belt fall to the ground and kept chatting, at the
same time moving round slowly, and ended up standing by the
belt. Without drawing attention to it he quietly kicked under a car.
Eventually the conversation came to an end and the customer left.
Sam came in laughing, saying, 'I wonder if he noticed?'

Another time a couple came and spent several hours down the
yard, and the Mrs was going in and out to their car fetching tools.
Mother was sent to watch them, and noticed that they were taking
wheels and tyres across the yard and putting them in the hedge
in the next field. When they eventually came to pay for what they
had, Sam climbed over the hedge and sat with the wheels and
waited. He didn't have to wait long. The woman had placed the
tyres so all she had to do was put her arm through the hedge and
pull them out. Sam was waiting, so when he saw her hand he
grabbed it. He said, 'She didn't half scream, I didn't let her go
though.' He told her she could pay or he would call the police.
He charged her twice the normal amount.

RABBIT IN A KETTLE

You know when you meet people in life and they tell you how
they knew your Father and how their father and your Father were
great friends? I met a man called Roland Saffin, who once told
me a story about how his father and Sam had been out working
together and ended up in the pub half the day and half the night.
When they had managed to get back to the scrapyard they were
both hungry. Old man Saffin asked Sam if he had anything to
eat. Sam said he didn't have anything to eat apart from a rabbit.
Sam couldn't find anything to cook the rabbit in; all he had was a
kettle, so they boiled the rabbit in the kettle.

Young Roland Saffin met Sam one day and Sam had told him how he'd been drinking with his father and ended up having rabbit cooked in a kettle. Roland said to Sam, 'Was the rabbit good then?' Sam replied, 'Yeah it was good, but the bones got stuck in the spout.'

SAM AT THE ROUND UP

Father knew a farmer called Christopher Beeson, who lived out on Long Lane near Manaton. Mr Beeson had grazing rights on a common called Easdon. Father made a deal to run his ponies on the common in exchange for half the profits gained from selling the colts. It was a walled-in common, very hilly, full of rocks, and covered in bracken with the odd patch of gorse. You couldn't ever see the ponies very well, just the tops of their ears moving, and you'd hear them rustling through the bracken. There was a gate that led straight from the common to Mr Beeson's farm. The idea was to round up the ponies and drive them along the wall to the open gate that led down to the farmyard. Sounds easy…

It was about the first week in October. Mother and my brothers and two workmen were on foot; I was riding a black mare called Beauty. We were to gather the ponies while Father stood by the gate, as he was too heavy and too old to run. We all spread out, disappearing into the bracken looking for the ponies and trying to gather them into a group.

Quietly we started to guide them along the wall towards the gate. Just as we were approaching it Father came out from behind a bush, waving his stick and hanky while blowing raspberries. He did this thinking it would turn them down towards the gate. However, he would only spook them into stampeding back towards the common. We cursed him; this happened every year. We then had to try and get in front of them and turn them back. At this point they would be running in all directions and very wary of us.

On one occasion Tim our workman took off after one, running downhill. You could just see his head and shoulders bobbing above the dense bracken as he chased after it. He was just gaining on it when all of a sudden he disappeared and the pony galloped out of sight. After a while Tim reappeared limping.

Tom Endacott's farm, Gidleigh, cleared by the Harris family in 1985
after Tom's death © *Chris Chapman*

He had fallen into a hole and badly winded and bruised himself. He gave it up as a bad job.

The rest of us gathered them up and – just like before – Father spooked them. He never learned and always caused a lot of bad language. I shot off after them on Beauty. Heading up on them up the steep hill we were about to turn them when she lost her footing. She landed on her nose, while I fell off over her head. She had banged her knee and was lame. I gave up and went home, leaving even more bad language behind.

FAIR PRICES

There was a time someone came and asked Sam how much something was. Sam stated his price and the customer wanted to knock the price down. So Sam told the chap, 'I haven't got what you want,' even though he was stood right beside it. Sam prided himself on his fair prices. He didn't like piss-takers!

Family Life

A Customer Commented

A customer commented on how it never hurt us kids growing up on the scrapyard with all the dirt. He said he remembered seeing Jim, my eldest brother, when he was a toddler cutting his teeth on an old radiator rubber hosepipe. He said Jim's face was black from the rubber hose he'd been chewing on.

Top and Tail

Up until we were about ten years old my twin Bob and I used to sleep 'top and tail' in a single caravan bed, two foot wide. He used to sleep under the gas light near the bucket toilet at one end, and I was under the built-in cupboard at the other. It was quite cramped, but not too bad in winter. As we grew bigger and our legs grew longer it became less comfortable. One night Bob and I started to kick each other and he scratched me with his toenail and in a minute we were squabbling loudly. The next thing we knew Mother came marching in with a big wet brick she had found outside. She lifted the bedcovers and put the wet brick between us and said in a shirty tone, 'Kick that!' That brick stayed in the bed for a long time.

Meals

Mother was a lousy cook. She would always cook the same old things. We mainly ate belly pork with boiled potatoes that still had their skins on. She said she never had any time to peel them, plus you got all the goodness out of them. Customers would give us swedes, turnips, kale or stringy beans. Once a week we would have sausages, sometimes a shoulder of lamb for Sundays, with roast potatoes still in their skins and tinned peas and carrots.

Father would kill a chicken if things were tight. He would pluck it indoors in a cardboard box and get feathers everywhere, or outside in the summer. He would draw it on newspaper on the dining table. The guts stank; he put me off eating chicken by watching him. Sometimes he would have duck that had been running around outside. Father loved to eat the giblets and the duck's feet for supper.

Jim, Bob and Peggy, 1985 © *Chris Chapman*

Mother had goats so we had lots of goats' milk to drink, but I was never too keen on it. Mother was always making junket; Father loved it and so did she, and I hated it. It's a white, slimy, sourish milk, with a hint of nutmeg.

Us kids would always stock up on our school dinners during the week, as the primary school dinner ladies would give us three seconds and thirds. We were often sat in the dinner hall eating up all the leftovers. There was one dinner lady called Mrs Rice, an old lady who knew Father well. She would often say it was lovely to see children eat up so well. We were always starving, and the school meals were better than what we had at home. Our school dinner was our main meal for the day, as we would have beans on toast or soup and bread for tea.

I remember one time when I was about seven Mother put a bowl of soup in front of each of us, and went off to cut some bread. She came back and handed me the bread to pass to my brothers. Bob was sat beside me. I tried to rest a piece of bread on the edge of his bowl, but it slipped into his soup. He started to whinge, 'I didn't want my bread in my soup' in a loud voice. He thought I'd done it on purpose. Mother came thundering in; she clipped my ear, picked up the piece of soup-soaked bread and rubbed it into my face, scolding me for interfering.

STARTING SCHOOL

Bob started going to school a few months before me; the idea was to split us up as we were twins. We had never gone to playgroup, so we were very shy. When I started school I wanted to stick close to Bob. I shadowed him for days. After a couple of weeks the teachers wanted to move Bob to a different class, but I kicked up so much that they didn't part us and we were sent to the next class together. The other children would pick on us and make fun of us as their fathers had been up to our place for spares for their cars, or my Father had been to their place picking up scrap or old cars, or had been to someone's they knew.

Marbles were the 'in' things; everyone would play marbles at break time. There were lots of different coloured ones, big ones, small ones. I found my marbles in car batteries. I used to hunt the batteries for marbles, wash the acid off and the kids didn't know where I'd got them from. They thought they were very special, so everyone would want to play against me. The next hit was ball bearings; I would strip diffs out of back axles and out of Mini drive shafts. One day I took half a carrier bag full to school and I was famous: everyone wanted to play. They cheated like hell to win and would make up new rules, but I played with different kids for weeks. But when the ball bearings were gone, so were they.

The kids would laugh at my haircut. Mother would cut my hair, and she used to keep it cut short. She would put an old riding hat on my head and cut around it.

Mother would lead Bob and I out on Donkey Jack to the main road to catch the bus if we were early enough. One winter Father had bought a box of large apples for us. Mother would cut two apples in half and wrap half in tissue paper ready for our morning break. I remember taking them out of my coat pocket at break time. The tissue would be all brown from the apple juice. I would have to spend time picking off soggy brown tissue before any of the other kids saw, because you'd hear them saying, 'Yuk, look at her apple – it's bad, it's got dirty paper on it.' Brother had the same problem.

THE DAY WE MISSED THE MINIBUS

One day, just after we had started a new term, Bob and I were late and missed the minibus. As we were young then, Mother used to take us out to the main road to catch it. She decided to catch it up in her pink Austin A55. We had bought it the day before, taxed and roadworthy, off an old man. She sped through the narrow lanes, trying to catch up. We caught up with it when it was nearly down to Chagford, heading downhill. The children on the bus spotted us and told the driver Eric to stop. The bus stopped, but the car we were in wouldn't. The brakes failed and we went straight into the back of the minibus; everyone on board bumped their heads. I flew over the back seat and hit the dashboard, Bob fell onto the floor. Eric had lost the bobble of his bobble hat. No one was seriously hurt, but the minibus had to have a new back door and step.

TOOTH FAIRY

When Bob was about six he lost one of his first milk teeth, and put it under his pillow. The next morning he looked under his pillow and found ten pence. Beside that lay a big brown tooth. He grabbed the ten pence in one hand and the tooth in the other. He looked at it in amazement, wondering where it had come from. He went running to Father shouting, 'The fairy has left me a big tooth and ten pence!' 'Did she?' said Father, grinning. 'I should put that tooth back under your pillow, the fairy might come back tonight.'

Later that evening Bob put it back under his pillow. He didn't go to sleep for ages; he kept fidgeting as we shared the same bed. Eventually we both went to sleep. The next morning he found 50 pence under the pillow and the tooth had gone.

It was a cow's tooth that Father had found out of a skull that had come in an old scrap car. He laughed about it for years.

BEDTIME STORIES

Mother wasn't a tactile person, and never showed us kids she loved us. There wasn't any cuddles. But I do remember one winter when I was about seven she used to read to us every night, just before we went to bed. We had been given a box full of comics, and in the comics were the Brer Rabbit stories. So every night for several weeks Mother would turn up the oil lamp on the table to the brightest it would go and sit down and read one story. Father would sit quiet if he was in to listen, and occasionally would lean in and light a cigarette from the long lamp glass.

We would all sit around the table in the caravan, listening quietly. Attached to the window was a box with a flap on it; the phone was kept in it during the day so Father could answer it from outside. At that time we had a black-and-white tomcat called Thomas. He would use the phone box as a cat flap. The table was against the side of the caravan and the cat would sit or sleep behind the oil lamp, as it threw out a lot of heat. I remember when Mother was sat reading the cat would rattle his way through the phone box and would stroll to the back of the table. He would almost put his nose on the oil lamp so that sometimes you would hear his whiskers singe. He would settle down and listen along with us. I remember enjoying the stories, and when the story came to an end and we had to go to bed I couldn't wait until the next night. I was very disappointed when the box ran out because that was the last time Mother read to us.

HALLOWE'EN

Mother had a funny side to her occasionally. One year when we were very young she had trouble with her teeth and ended up with false ones. Hallowe'en came round and we sat having tea in lamplight. Mother was out in the kitchen, and decided to undo her bun and let down her long greying hair, right down to her waist – and drop her teeth out. She came through the caravan cackling like a witch. We were taken by surprise and I wanted to hide under the table as I had just turned six.

FIREWORKS

For bonfire night Father would collect all the rubbish from around the yard: old tyres, household furniture, car seats and rubber. He would have it all pushed into a heap, over ten foot high. Old Fred from up the road would buy us fireworks. Mother would keep them in a tin; it was her job to light them. Fireworks never lasted long; it was more fun watching the fire. There was every colour you could think of dancing in the bonfire. The tyres would explode and blow sparks into the night sky; they'd whistle and squeal, pop and bang. Flames would roar and leap out into the darkness.

RUBBED THEIR NOSES IN IT

Mother took no nonsense from anyone, and that went for the animals as well. I remember a day when she caught a cat that had shat on the floor. Out came the pepper pot; she dusted the pile while grabbing the cat by the scruff, forcing its nose to the pile. The cat resisted. Its feet were anchored to the ground, pushing back, as she dragged its nose down into it. She mopped the cat up in the rest of it before opening the door and throwing the cat out after she had given it a good scolding. You wouldn't see the cat for nearly a week. I tell you that cat never shat on the floor again. And as for a dog – well, she found it a lot harder, more of a struggle as she wrestled with it, trying to put its nose in it.

We once had some young part-grown ducklings running about the yard. At that time we had a young lurcher called Tike.

Mother let him off one morning for a run and he killed a couple of ducklings. Mother was so cross with him she decided to tie a dead duckling around the dog's neck, like a collar, until it started to stink. She thought she would cure the dog of killing anything again. All day the customers would ask, 'Why has that dog got a dead duck around his neck?' Being a lurcher Tike had a short bottom jaw, and that night he got the dead duckling off his neck and ate it.

One of our other dogs Patsy, a Springer spaniel, would pinch the chicken eggs. Mother decided to cure her of this. She got an egg and filled it up with mustard and forced the dog to eat it. It made her sick, but it never stopped her.

PACKED LUNCHES

We were out breaking up a large caravan on a farm. I was seven or eight years old, so it must have been during the holidays or one weekend. Bob and I were helping Cliffy (Janny Cliff) and Father break it up. They'd collected a load of scrap and Father was taking it home. He told us that he was going to bring some lunch back. I was left with Bob and Cliffy, and when they finished knocking up the caravan Cliffy made a fire to burn up the rubbish. As it was a hot sunny day Bob and I chased around the fields.

It was ages before Father came back. He had a basket in the lorry and handed it to us saying, 'Here's your lunch.' We took the basket and looking inside it; it was full of old shoes and a bottle of squash. We were very disappointed as we were hungry. But Father was having a good laugh; he fetched a biscuit tin from the lorry. It was full of doorstep sandwiches with great chunks of cheese with black thumbprints on them, as Father had made them himself. We sat on the grass watching the fire as we ate our sandwiches.

Sometimes we had school trips where we had to take a packed lunch. We hated taking a packed lunch as all the kids would have nice neat sandwiches, and ours would be doorsteps with a greasy cold fried egg and cold bacon poking out, or we'd have a boiled free-range egg that would stink and cause the kids to pass comments and move away. You wouldn't want Father to make the sandwiches either, as then you had to put up with black thumbprints as well.

Bad Eggs

Father used to have lots of chickens running around the place and they would lay their eggs out in the scrapyard, under wheel arches, inside the cars or under odd bits of scrap metal kicking around. Sometimes he didn't find them straight away.

We nearly always had eggs for breakfast and one morning Mother was in a temper. She had got fired up about something, and when she was like this we all kept our heads down. She gave me two boiled eggs, and told me to hurry up and eat my breakfast because we were running late for the school bus. The first egg tasted a bit funny but I daren't say anything to Mother, as she would have been quick to clip my ear. But when it came to the second egg I just couldn't eat it. When I took off the top I could see there was a dead chick in it! I wailed, 'I can't eat this!' Mother said, 'What's wrong with it?' and came over, ready to snap. Then she could see for herself. I said, 'The other one tasted bad too!' She said, 'You shouldn't have eaten it.'

I'm still very suspicious of free-range eggs!

TV

We got into a lot of mischief as we made our own fun. We didn't have a TV at home for a long time, but we watched television with a lady down the road called Helen. She let us watch her TV for years after school. Sometimes we would go over to Nan's after school and watch her set. Sometimes we got to see TV when Father picked up scrap from customers, but it was pot luck what programmes you saw – too often it was the news!

My eldest brother Jim bought his own TV and ran it on car batteries. He and Bob would watch TV on their own in the caravan and I wasn't allowed in, so I used to stand on the bumper of an old van and watch it through the window. I would stand there for hours in all weathers, even rain and frost. One day they were watching a comedy and I was laughing. Jim heard me and pulled the curtains shut and that was the end of that. He then kept the curtains permanently closed.

Later on there was a TV for everyone to watch but it too was run on car batteries, as we still had no mains electricity. Jim rigged up an engine on a dynamo to charge up the battery.

Father never wanted a TV, but whenever you went in he always had it turned on (and he soon learnt how to change channels).

COCONUTS AT THE CARNIVAL

One year Mother took us to the carnival in Moretonhampstead.
She let us go to the fair for a while before she had to get us back
home so Father could go to the pub for the night. That year, for
the first time ever, I won some coconuts. I asked Mother to hold
them while I went on the bumper cars. She told me to meet her
at the gate, so we could go home after the ride. After the bumper
cars I went to the gate, but Mother and my brothers weren't there.
I waited a while, then I panicked; I thought they had gone on
without me. I ran all the way out of Moretonhampstead, just over
a mile, but when I got to the car they weren't there. So I ran back
again. I knew Mother would be wicked. I got back to the fair and
she was so annoyed she gave my coconuts away, and shoved me in
the back of the car. I was about eight at the time.

Bob (Peggy's twin) and Sam, 1980 © *Chris Chapman*

44

PLAYING DRAUGHTS WITH FATHER

We were rummaging through the jumble one Saturday evening when I was about eight and I found a draughts board. I asked Father what game was played on this board. He told me it was a draughts board and if I found the pieces he would show me how to play. I looked through the boxes and couldn't find any. Father told me old buttons would do. We needed 24, 12 white and 12 black. That evening Father showed me how to play draughts.

BEATEN EGGS

When we were young Mother would often beat free-range eggs that she found around the yard with sugar and watered-down Carnation Milk or goats' milk. Some eggs would taste stronger than others; I guess it depended on how old they were.

You knew when it was coming because you could hear her beating it in the kitchen. It would look all pale and frothy and slimy at the bottom. She would make us drink it for breakfast every morning for years. The eggs would taste strong and slimy and a bit gritty sometimes; she told us it was good for us. Mother took up ordering herbal pills and vitamins so we would have to have several brownish-green pills with the beaten egg.

I would end up burping eggs all morning; the kids at school accused me of having bad breath. When I told Mother the kids at school were teasing me she started to give me garlic pills and told me to tell them to smell that! Garlic was much better than eggy breath.

AUNTY ANGEL

I spent a couple of summers on my Nan and grandfather's farm at Lingcombe, just over the fields from home. My grandfather didn't think a scrapyard was a place for a girl. I spent at least two summers there with my cousin Kirsty, who was two years younger than me.

My Aunty Angel worked and lived on the farm. She milked the cows and fed the young calves and checked the sheep. I remember her dragging long branches home from the fields and cutting them up for firewood, ready for the winter. She would walk around the fields digging up thistles and stopping up gaps in the hedges, where the sheep had escaped. Her two collie dogs, Bryan and Missie, went everywhere with her.

Nan used to get Angel to look after us after dinner. Her idea was to wear us out, so she'd take us for long walks with the two dogs. We would walk up over the moor and go to the river and paddle. I remember going whortleberry picking with Aunty Angel, Kirsty and Nan. We rode in her little blue Austin A35 to the moor near the Warren House Inn. There were lots of whort bushes there. We would spend hours picking little berries one by one, putting them in plastic boxes, eating a few and getting blue fingers and tongue.

What really stands out in my mind was one summer when I was about nine years old. We would walk around the fields and find feathers: pigeon feathers, buzzards, crows and magpies. I remember talking about how the Indians wore feathers and how the big chief had a big headdress. Aunty Angel said she could make one of them when we had enough feathers, so Kirsty and I collected more feathers from the chickens. Aunty Angel found an old brown shirt that was her father's or brother's. She cut it up and made a long strip; she sewed it with her old Singer sewing machine and fitted around our heads. Then she cut slits in it and placed all the feathers in it so that it looked like a real headdress. We played with it for the rest of that summer.

GOING TO SECONDARY SCHOOL

I found it hard when I started secondary school. We had to catch two buses; we had to go down the lane about a quarter of a mile to catch the minibus. The kids who rode on that bus were mainly farming children. We all stood around in Chagford and waited for the big coach. This was where the two buses arrived, one to pick up the village children and the other coach to take the children who came in on minibuses from around Chagford. Waiting in the village would be where trouble would start. Kids would think it was right to pick on you because you were different. They would kick your bag around and toss it to one another.

One day a boy decided that I needed a wash, so he went into the gents' toilets and fetched a bucket of water. It was a cold winter morning; he came out and threw it over me. I was soaked. I felt I couldn't go home so I caught the minibus to my Nan's place and spent the day drying out.

It was hard just to ride on the minibus. It had wooden bench seats running down both sides, with an iron arm in the middle of the seat.

We all seemed to sit in the same places. I had to sit with the iron bar on my lefthand side, with three or four big lads sat to my right. They thought it was fun to ram you into the bar every time the bus stopped. They would exaggerate the stopping motion of the bus. Sometimes it would knock the wind out of me, sometimes they would leave me bruised. I learnt to watch where we were going and be ready for the bus to stop. I would jump out of my seat and leave them to pile in on the next one to me, who didn't think it was funny.

MOUSTACHE

When in her fifties my Mother was doing a man's work. Driving and loading her vehicle, on her own or with one of us kids. One Saturday Father, Mother and I went to Moretonhampstead to pick up scrap from one of the council houses. We had loaded up, Mother was driving, and I was sat in the middle. We were heading to Chagford to pick up some more. As we were just leaving Moreton, Father told Mother that she worked like a man. I was about 12 at the time and, without thinking, I said, 'Yes you do, you're growing a moustache like one too!' With that she gave me a 'back hander' across the mouth and nose, which caused me to bang my head on the back window. All Father could do was laugh his head off. He took up most of the seat and as he laughed he pushed me into Mother, who wasn't best pleased with me (and that was the last place I wanted to be). The air was like thunder.

JAY'S GRAVE

It was very rare that Father and Mother would go out together. On one occasion they went out visiting friends at Ashburton. They left late and headed back across over the moor. They had to pass Jay's Grave. Just before they passed the grave Mother said, 'Touch your hat, Father', out of respect for the dead. As she said this she lifted the back of his cap. He nearly jumped out of the van; he thought it was Jay's ghost. This made Mother laugh.

MOTHER DISAPPEARING

When I was eight-and-a-half years old Mother disappeared. She didn't tell me she was leaving; I woke up one Saturday and she had gone. I asked my eldest brother where she was, and he told me she had left home. I couldn't understand it. I spent the whole weekend shouting and looking for her. Then Jim said she had gone over the fields. After a week she came and found me: she must have heard me shouting. She said she needed time to herself and she was camping under the stars. She was living off bread and cheese and drinking river water. She took me down over the fields to where her camp was, and I saw that she was still doing the books for the business.

She left again about three years later and she didn't just go over the fields. She dropped me off at the Ardens, where I was helping at the riding stables. Then she just drove off. I didn't know where she was going, or if she was coming back. I just got on with my day; I was going to a horse show. When I got back from the show, and it was time to go home, it hit me. I turned pale, and Johnny Arden could see I wasn't well. That's when it all came to a head: he asked me if I was hurt. I just broke down and blurted out that my Mum had gone. He couldn't believe it and took me home.

Father found out where Mother was and took me to see her. He used me to get her to come home. She was down in Ashburton with some friends. He got me to plead with her, and he said to her, 'Just come home for the weekend, and I will bring you back on Monday.' She agreed, but he never took her back to Ashburton. She wasn't happy for years; she said she'd leave again when she was 60.

GOING TO THE DENTIST

We were late for a dentist appointment; us three kids were squeezed in the front of an Austin J4. Mother was driving; we had to go to Newton Abbot, about 12 miles from Moretonhampstead. As we left Moreton we caught up with the local bus. The road was very windy. We went over the rise past Wray Barton, then over the little humped-back bridge, passing the duck barn in the field (before this section of the road was straightened). The road was two-lane but narrow, and there was a blind bend ahead. Mother was worked up; she never liked to be late for anything. She made up her mind she was going to pass the bus. She pulled out alongside it and we could see the bus was just about to go round the blind bend, but Mother was determined to pass and was pushing her foot further to the floor. The van engine was roaring; we looked at each other in silence. I held my breath and I think we all shut our eyes as Mother roared round the outside of the bus. We could hear the hedge hitting Mother's wing mirror. It was tight, and luckily for us there wasn't anything coming the other way.

MY BIRTHDAY

On my thirteenth birthday Mother gave me a present; this was a first. She usually gave me money; I was so pleased to have a present. It was in a brown paper bag. I opened it and pulled it out: a packet of Doctor Whites. I didn't know what it was or what it was for. I asked Mother; she said: 'Just put it away somewhere safe, you'll need it one day.' I thought it was an odd present, so I just put it away. Six months later I started my period, and I thought I was dying. All Mother said was, 'You still got your birthday present?' 'Yes,' I said, bewildered. 'Well, slap one between your legs and change it regular' – and that was it.

BURNT

Every Saturday Father had seven or eight cars lined up in a row on their sides to burn out. They would burn out and cool down ready for Monday morning so that the workmen could cut them up for baling. The cars had to be burnt or they would have caught alight when the men were cutting them up with gas torches, and in those days there wasn't any legislation to stop you burning out old cars. We used to bale all light iron back in the seventies because it was the easiest way to move it.

Father had seven cars all lined up, ready to burn. He used to light a piece of foam rubber and walk down the line of cars, throwing a piece into each. Then he would walk back up the line, making sure each one was thoroughly alight before making his way back home.

This day he had some old cars that had been in the yard for some time. They had all been well stripped of their spare parts and were ready to go. As he walked back through – as he had done many times before – there was an explosion. He was caught in the blast and showered in burning petrol. He was a walking ball

of fire. If Janny Cliff our workman hadn't rugby tackled him to the floor and rolled him on the ground to put out the flames he would have been burnt to death. What made things worse was the fact that Father was wearing nylon overalls, which burnt easily and stuck to him.

He had very serious burns. Cliffy helped him up to the caravan which we were living in. Father went into shock; he was shaking so much he made the caravan rattle. He was lucky he hadn't burnt his face. His peaked cap had saved him; the petrol had run down the peak and missed his face. The flames dripped down two inches in front of his face, like curtains, so his eyes and face were saved from serious damage.

Mother should have called for an ambulance, but Father was too afraid to go to the hospital. Instead she called the doctor, but our own doctor was away and she spoke to a locum, an Austrian doctor here for the summer. It was 5.30pm and he told Mother to bathe my father, put him in clean bed clothes and bring him to the surgery by 6.30pm because that was when the surgery closed.

Mother couldn't bathe him because we didn't have a bath, so she set about to wash him and pull off his clothes. Bear in mind that his overalls were an all-in-one boiler suit and made of nylon, which had melted and stuck to his legs. She didn't have time to get him ready to take to the surgery so she put him to bed.

Us kids could hear him scream from across the yard. That night he kept me awake all night because he was shaking and my room was next to his. I could hear him groaning in pain and he made the caravan tremble.

The next day the doctor arrived and was in with Father for a long time. The doctor told Mother that Father needed to go to the burns unit in Bristol as he had third degree burns, and if they didn't kill him the shock might. But Father refused to go and Mother was left to nurse him. The doctor came regularly and brought dressings, which Mother had to change every day. It made Father scream and shout and swear; he was in agony.

Mother decided that the dressings were no good and as she used to study herbs she decided to treat him herself. She used honey, plantain leaves and comfrey, and after three months in bed Father's leg had healed.

Sam at Lettaford, photographed soon after the burning incident in 1977
Courtesy of Peggy Harris

DRUNK ON MANGOLD WINE

Father, Jim, Bob and Cliffy went to Chagford to pick up some scrap from John Meredith. He had made some homemade wine. He made it from mangolds, a root grown for cattle feed, a bit like a swede.

Father tasted it and said it was all right, so they all drank it. Another round came and Jim and Cliffy tipped theirs away down the drain. Bob, who was youngest, had three or four small glasses. After a while John was well gone and suggested that Jim drive his little red sports car around Chagford. Father said, 'He can't do that!'

'He'll be alright!' said John, so Jim drove it round the village, luckily safely. Then they came back and had another round. Jim and Cliffy were still tipping theirs down the drain, but Father was enjoying his and having got the taste decided that he would go down to The Globe for a brown ale to top it off. The landlord said. 'You alright Sam? You look rough, what you been up to?'

Father said that he had been drinking mangold wine with John. The landlord said, 'Cor, you don't want to drink that stuff, it's dangerous!'

Father drank up and said, 'Cheerio!' and walked out of the door, but when the fresh air hit him he was out cold. When Cliffy and Jim found him he wasn't fit to stand up. Cliffy couldn't drive and Jim was too young, but they decided that Cliffy would sit in the driver's seat and Jim would sit on his lap and this way Jim would drive home down the narrow lanes.

They couldn't get Father into the cab so they rolled him, with some difficulty, into the back of the pick-up. They had trouble at first even getting him onto his feet as he was a heavy man and his legs didn't work. On the way home they had Bob throwing up in the cab, and Father trying to get up in the back. Every time he tried to stand up Jim would do an emergency stop and he would fall down again. They didn't want him to fall over the side, and this was the only way they could keep him down.

Mother and I were at home and she was getting a little worried as to where they had got to when they arrived. Bob was an interesting shade of green and couldn't stop throwing up, and it took all of us to get Father in to bed as he was not the lightest man and the caravan we lived in at the time was long with a narrow corridor.

They all suffered for days and it put Father off the booze for weeks!

DRIVING WITH MY FATHER

When I was 18 we bought a red pick-up from the landlord of the Three Crowns in Chagford. It was in very good condition, but after a while a crack appeared over the passenger's wheel arch. I used to drive this vehicle the most. Father would ride around with me; I would tell him not to press his boot down on the wheel arch as he would make the hole bigger, but he ignored me. He would push his boot down to push himself back into the seat. Of course he made the hole worse, so I had to avoid puddles or the passenger would get wet.

One day Father annoyed me; we had to go out, but I didn't know where to. I turned the pick-up round ready to go. Father got in and I asked, 'Where we going?' He replied, 'You know.' 'No, I don't!' 'To whatdyacall? You know!' 'No; no idea.' He would often say stupid things like this, like I should know. So I drove off, annoyed with him, hoping he would direct me. He didn't like it as I was driving over 30mph, which he never did. He started calling me an idiot. That really got my goat. As I was driving along I saw some horseshit so I lined up the passenger wheel and drove through it. Father got covered. He started shouting more, so I lined up some puddles and everything nasty. He would see it coming and start protesting, furiously. He would curse me and I told him he stank!

THE DAY THE DOOR FELL OFF

I could drive before I had a licence; I learnt to drive on the road in a grey transit van, with sliding doors. One day the local policeman stopped me in Chagford to ask if we had any parts for a car. He pulled my door open to speak, and it dropped off in his hand and crashed to the floor. He was a bit surprised. I hopped out, lifted the door and replaced it, answered his question and drove off.

GETTING INTO SCRAPES

PETROL FIX

When I was about five or six I would go round sniffing petrol tanks and get very high. I just loved two-star petrol; the fumes would make me hallucinate. The trees would talk to me and gas cylinders lying on the ground would open up and turn into red-hot snapping monsters. I would run around yelling and jump over them. It felt as if my feet were on fire. I would go on until the effect wore off or I passed out. When Mother eventually noticed what I was doing, she cured me for good. She gave me the hiding of a lifetime.

After that I learned not to sniff but to siphon petrol instead. We siphoned petrol from the cars to be scrapped so it could be reused, and to prevent accidents if the cars were burnt, as we did in those days. When we were older we used the petrol in our mopeds and cars, but when I was young I used to sell it for pocket money. I would sell it to people who came to the yard for spare parts.

There were some young lads who used to come from Princetown on a regular basis to buy cars or parts. They were a bunch of rogues and you had to watch them. They often bought petrol off me, five gallons at a time, each week. One week they put some petrol in the car and then said that they didn't have any money but would pay me next week. Next week came and went, and the following weekend too. Then they turned up and told me they had been and paid Mother. I knew they hadn't, and they wanted more petrol. I said, 'Money up front!' and they paid up. I went and got ropey petrol and peed in the top of the can. It all looks the same colour, but sinks nicely to the bottom of the car's petrol tank and eventually stops the car. You have to drain the system to get things going again.

I had great pleasure imagining their journey home across the moor. That taught them for trying to cheat me!

Sam weighing copper scrap, 1986 © *Chris Chapman*

STUCK UP A TREE

I used to climb up the tree by the entrance to the scrapyard. Father hung a piece of rope from a branch for his scales so he could weigh the customers' scrap.

One evening the local policeman from Moretonhampstead came to have a chat with Father. I must have been about six; I wasn't very big. The policeman got out of his police car, an old Morris 1000 with a white box on the roof with the word 'Police' on it and a blue light on top. He looked at me and said, 'I bet you can't climb that tree', as I was stood at the base of it. I said, 'I can climb it! I've climbed right to the top several times before.' I took off climbing the same route that I had done many times. This time one of the branches snapped, but that didn't stop me from going right to the top. I looked down and shouted to the policeman, 'See I can climb right to the top!' But the problem started when I began to climb back down. I got to the broken branch and couldn't reach the next one; I tried several times. I shouted down, 'I can't get down!' Father shouted up, 'Come on, get down!' I started crying. So the policeman took off his hat and jacket and climbed up and rescued me.

RAFT

One day a raft that had been used in the River Dart raft race came in the scrap. It was made out of 12 plastic five-gallon drums, bound in a steel frame with three seats. My brother Jim took it down to the pond on the bottom of the scrapyard and we all played on it. It stayed there for the winter, and by the next summer the boys had taken it to Stiniel Down and put it in the river. When I rode round on horseback I would see other children playing on the raft. They'd found it tied up under the bridge.

My brother Jim and his mate took the raft upriver to Green Combe valley just two fields from home. They dammed up the river and made a pond. It was hot that summer and the river became warm; I remember swimming in it. Up in the hill under a tree was a hole, an old mineshaft. Jim and his mate Rob took the raft and squeezed it into the small hole. The shaft went back into the hill; they would run an old car battery and headlight and use it for light. Just by the entrance the water was ankle deep, but was deeper within feet. They spent hours floating along the shaft.

I often went in and floated the raft there. I remember the earthy smell; it was very cold, dark and damp. We used a long stick to push the raft back and forth; when we got to the end you couldn't touch the bottom. I found it a bit spooky.

DRIVING

How many kids get to drive old cars around? We could; we had a mile of lane to drive up and down, safely off the proper road. We would tie a sledge or an old car bonnet behind the car and pull each other round the field on it. We called it 'grass surfing'.

Hide and seek was good in a scrapyard too, but it was never easy to find anyone with three acres of scrap cars to search.

I started to learn to drive a car by steering in the scrap cars. Dave Leaman, our workman, would push the old car with an old Chaseside tractor, a big machine with forks on the front. It had no brakes, and he would set you off with a big bump up the back of the car and send you rolling down the lane. When you got to the bottom he would give you another shove. The tractor was like a roaring, steaming monster, and it used to frighten me. I would worry about whether the big forks would come through the boot of the car. Dave pushed you and shouted out over the roaring noise where he wanted you to steer. If you didn't go where he

Dave and Gwen Leaman, 1979 © *Chris Chapman*

wanted he would lift the back of the car on the fork and push it where he wanted you to go.

Dave worked for us for many years. He always wore a woolly hat and we kids thought he was like a cow; he had no teeth and could lick his nose with his tongue!

STINK BOMBS

We used to play in the barns up at Lettaford, which were full of hay. Mrs Harvey's chickens used to lay in the barn opposite. It was an ideal nesting place for chickens. If Mrs Harvey didn't find the eggs for a while they went off. The barns were on the edge of a lane, which was used as a footpath. We could look out from under the roof, on top of the hay, and watch people walk by without being seen. We would use the bad eggs as missiles, and as they were full of gas they would explode with a loud 'Pop!' when they landed next to the hikers. The poor hikers would look round to see where they had come from, then pinch their noses and rush on saying, 'Bad eggs! Did you see where they came from?' They never stayed to investigate!

SLEDGING

One day we had spent hours going down one track and had made it very slippery and fast, as the snow had compacted down into ice. I went down it on my fertiliser sack headfirst, holding the corners of my sack up in front of me. When I got to the bottom I couldn't stop and went straight through the hedge and down a two-foot drop into the icy stream. I tell you I have never been that cold before or since!

OLD BULLETS

Sometimes there would be the odd 12-bore cartridge in the old cars, as some of them came from farms. If us kids found them when we were younger Father would put them in an old rabbit hole. As we got older we had our own air guns and used to get a lot of used ammunition from the military firing ranges. The ranger would bring sandbags full of fired blanks, and Father and I would empty the bags slowly into a wheelbarrow looking for the odd live shell. These were bullets that hadn't been fired. We had to check every bag and re-bag them before selling them on. Me and Jim would push the live bullets into the hedge with the firing pin showing and would fire at them with our air guns until we hit them and they would go 'Bang!' in the hedge. Great fun!

GRANDAD

My brother Bob was out collecting cars from a farm. He had been to the same farm several times, picking up two cars at a time. This afternoon he brought back an old Mini on the back of his truck and pulled behind him an old Peugeot that had been in an accident, which was why it was being scrapped.

We always looked through the cars for anything of value, money, tools or anything. I noticed a square box behind the seat of the Peugeot. I spotted it at the same time as my brother Jim, but I got there first. I lifted the box out and noticed a square brass plaque on the top with a name and dates on it. I realised what it was and handed it over to Jim, saying, 'You can have it, it's a casket.' 'A what?' Jim said, taking it. 'I don't want it.' He was about to throw it and I said, 'Don't do that, it's someone's Grandad.'

I told Bob he would have to take it back. He said, 'Alright, put it on the front seat of the truck. I'm going back there tomorrow.' I said, 'You'll have to be careful with it, it's leaking and if you stop quick you will get Grandad up your nose.'

'Oh, bugger,' he said, 'don't put it in there then.' I said, 'You must take it back, it belongs to the people where you got the car from. I tell you what I'll do, I'll put Grandad in a fertiliser sack and if he comes out of his box he won't get up your nose.'

Next day Bob took Grandad back to his family. He stood at the front door with Grandad in a blue fertiliser sack. The granddaughter answered the door, and Bob told her that he only took dead cars, not Grandads, and handed her the sack. She said, 'Oh, I wondered where he was. We must have forgotten to take him out of the car after the accident!'

THE GRENADE

When I was about eight or nine I found a grenade out at Gidleigh Castle when we were given the job of clearing out the old tin sheds. The grenade was left over from the Second World War, and I was told it had been disarmed. It was black and lay in my hand like a baby pineapple. It looked alive as it still had the lever and the pin.

My brothers and I had good fun with it, frightening everyone who came to the scrapyard. When the customers were busy taking spare parts off the cars down we would creep up on them and quietly roll the grenade behind the car and shout 'Grenade!' We would sit back and watch them run and take cover, then we'd begin to laugh and go and pick it up. Sometimes the customers would shout at us to take cover as they thought it was still alive. Others would call us 'Stupid buggers'.

The best way to wind them up was to walk up to them when they were busy and ask them what it was you were holding. They would turn round, happy to answer. They would either take one look, gasp, grab it and throw it as far as they could, or panic and leg it, or freeze.

One day I threw it over a car and it fell into many pieces and that was the end of it. Fun over until the next thing came along!

Jim being pushed by Pete Northway on a homemade go-kart, 1978 © *Chris Chapman*

GALLOPED OVER AT CHAGFORD SHOW

When I was about ten I went to Chagford Show for the first time. It was a hot August day and I rode a little black Dartmoor pony called Peter. I went to the show with the Ardens, as Peter was their pony. Clare and I lead the ponies round and watched different classes, as we were only riding in the gymkhana games. They were running late in the afternoon. The games were very fast, and I don't remember which games I entered – but for one.

The Ardens were ready to go home and there was one game left, the egg and spoon race. They told me to come home straight after it. I remember lining up in a row with about five others on their ponies. Spoon in hand and egg rocking, we were all told not to hold the spoons with our thumbs. The man at the side waved his handkerchief: 'Go!' Ponies lunged forwards and someone banged into me and my egg fell to the ground. So I got off to pick it up again. Peter was a little impatient and galloped over me as I was stooped over. I remember his front legs banging into me.

The next thing I knew I was in an ambulance with strange faces looking down at me and someone trying to put a bandage around my head and face. Peter had stood on my face and knocked me out. I freaked! They were talking about taking me to hospital, but I wasn't going there. I had to take Peter back straight after the race. Where was he? I remember shouting at the ambulance people, 'Where's my pony! I've got to take him home.' They reassured me Peter was fine and someone was going to take him home. I demanded I wanted Peter. So they took me to a horsebox where he was already loaded. This big man, who looked like a farmer, was standing on the ramp. He said, 'I'm taking the pony home.' I didn't know this man. I told him I wanted the pony, as I needed to take him home and if he didn't let me have Peter I was going to call the police. With this he grabbed me and pinned me over his knee and spanked me.

My head was thumping and my arse was stinging and I was crying on the horsebox ramp. I heard someone say, 'Alright Peg?' It was Mother; she came walking around the corner of the box to take me home as someone had phoned her. She told me that Mr Parr, the man who had just spanked me, was going to take Peter back to the Ardens as he knew them. The ambulance people suggested to Mother she should take me to see a doctor if I wasn't any better in the morning.

Mother took me home and walked me down to the river and picked some leaves off a bush growing there. She said, 'These are alder leaves, very good for swelling.' The left side of my face was very swollen. Mother would walk me to the river and change the leaves twice a day for about a week. I had to have the leaves bandaged around my face. I remember feeling sick, and my head thumped for days. I don't know if the leaves helped with the swelling or if time was the healer.

CAR KNOCKED ME DOWN

It was the Easter holidays; I was 12 years old. Our step-cousin Kimble came over on his new bike that he'd had for his birthday in February. He was very proud of it. He came to play with the kids from down the road. They were all taking it in turns to drive an old Hillman Minx that had come in for scrap round the field. My brother Jim was teaching them to drive.

I could drive already so I was sitting on the hedge watching them take it in turns. I was looking at Kim's bike – it was shining. All the chrome was like a mirror; you could see your face in the handlebars. It was light blue, three-speed and had a shiny bell. I fancied a ride on it as I'd never seen or ridden on a new bike.

I asked Kim if I could have a ride around the field. 'OK, but don't damage it, it's my new bike,' he replied unwillingly. He obviously didn't want me to ride it but he couldn't really say no as he was driving our car. 'I won't,' I replied. I jumped on it and was riding up and down the middle of the field, trying the gears, as they were all driving around the outside.

I noticed Kim was having his turn at driving. I glanced up and saw he was coming across the middle of the field, driving straight at me. I went to get out of his way but slipped on the pedals in the rush. He hit me sideways on and pushed me down the field. I shouted, 'Stop!' He did.

I started to stand up but he panicked and the car took off again, pushing me down the field. My face was being pushed along the grass, with the bike on top of me. My leg was trapped under the bumper; the bike was tangled around me. All I could see was the tyre coming closer and all I could hear was the engine roaring and in the distance the others shouting. At this point I was screaming 'Stop!' I could feel my body being pulled in. I was struggling, fighting against the pull. My face was burning, I could smell the rubber; I was getting pushed into the ground. The tyre was getting closer and closer, I struggled to hold my head back. The car stopped.

I lay there; the tyre was touching my face. If Kim hadn't stopped he would have driven over my head. I had lost my shoe up under the suspension. I had grass burns all over the right side of my body. The back of my ear felt like it was on fire. Jim pulled me out.

Everyone was panicking; Kim was crying and I was screaming. Jim slapped me across the face and told me to shut up. I told them I was going to tell Mother. Everyone was scared of our Mother, so was I. Jim was afraid that they would all get into trouble and told me I was to tell Mother that I had fallen off the bike coming down the lane. He went out into the lane and picked up a handful of dirt and rubbed it into my face to cover up the grass stains, and told everyone to say that I had fallen off the bike in the lane. So I couldn't tell Mother what had really happened, as she wouldn't have believed me.

Kim was scared stiff that his Mother would find out. I never told anyone, but when Kim was about 34, on his wedding day, he just had to tell his Mum his long-kept secret. He made a joke of it; it was a funny thing that happened in his childhood. He made me feel like I was just a joke.

Catching Fish

Clare Arden and I often used to ride past Batworthy Farm where Joe White and his sister Annie lived. Joe would come out to talk to us and admire the ponies, as we would ride different ones. He would comment on how they were improving, as they were often youngsters that had not long been broken.

Joe would take snuff out of a small blue box and sniff it up his nose. You could tell he enjoyed his snuff as there were little blue boxes scattered along the stone wall around his farmyard. Alongside the wall ran a small stream, and as we sat on the ponies talking you could see fish swimming in the water. I said to Joe one day, 'I can catch fish with my hands.' Joe smiled and laughed. 'You can have a go, the water's deeper in the field, behind the shed,' he said in disbelief.

So Clare and I went down one afternoon. I walked along the stream and watched to see where the fish darted in under the bank. I rolled up my sleeves and laid down on the bank and gently put my hand under, between the stones, and felt for the fish. When I felt one it would flap in my hand. I would grab tight and pull it out. I shouted, 'I got one Joe!' Joe was laughing and told me I was to go and show Annie. Annie laughed; she couldn't believe I caught it. 'I was watching, I didn't think she would catch one either,' replied Joe. Annie asked me what I was going to do with it. I told her I was going to take it home for Father to fry up for his supper. He ate it with a bit of bread and butter.

I went fishing several times and one time in my favourite spot Joe had placed a rat trap. He had caught a rat and drowned it in the stream. It looked like it had been there for a few days. Yuk!

HORSEPLAY

Clare and I used to play Cowboys and Indians on horseback. We would race around the woods where there were cross-country fences, and splash in and out of the river. We would plague the campers on Stiniel Down. We would ride up quietly, pull their guy-ropes up then charge off. Then we'd sneak back to watch them struggle out of their collapsed tent and would gallop off laughing. We would pinch their milk, cooling in the river, share it and put the bottle back empty.

When we rode over the common or the moor we would come across young lovers. Clare and I would charge past, hupping

and hollering. This would frighten the hell out of them. They would be grabbing clothes and trying to cover up. We wicked little girls thought this was good fun!

Holidaymakers often got lost in the country lanes. When they saw kids on ponies they thought we were locals and would give them directions. They were wrong. We would tell them to 'go straight on, turn left, then take the next left, go on a mile and take the next left' and send them on their way. We would set off in the opposite direction and wait to see them coming round full circle. We'd give a friendly wave or a thumbs up as they went by, then rush off before they stopped.

Liz Arden chatting to Joe White at Batworthy Farm, 1980 © *Chris Chapman*

Clare and I would go on the scrounge. I was always hungry, and as she was young she got away with it. Her first port of call was her Aunty Margaret, who wasn't her real aunty. We would get chocolate biscuits and cake. Sometimes she would go next door at the same time; it depended on how much we got from Aunty Margaret. Next was Mrs Hutchings and she would give us biscuits too.

It was always good to call round home on Saturday afternoon after the baker had been because we could get a biscuit from there, and around tea-time we could get a biscuit from the old man who lived next door to Clare. He usually gave us two custard creams. Sunday afternoon it was always busy at home with Father seeing to the customers, and if he knew Clare was with me he would give us 10p each to go up to the ice-cream van. So we did very well. You'd think we had worms – well actually I did!

Broken Down

One winter evening Mother and Father were out picking up metals from a regular customer at South Zeal. Me and my two brothers were at home. It was late and we'd gone to bed; the phone rang and I answered it. It was Mother; the van had broken down near Factory Bridge, just the other side of Chagford. Mother had gone to the nearest house to use the phone. She asked me to ask Jim to come and fetch them in the Austin J4. I went and asked Jim if he would go and pick them up.

He had gone to bed, and said 'No' as he only had a provisional licence. It was late; Father was in his early sixties and it was an uphill walk most of the way home. So I decided to go and fetch them myself. I was 14 and I could drive. I decided to dress up like Mother, so I put on a big coat, a peaked cap and a pair of glasses. I thought if anyone saw me they would just think I was Mrs Harris.

So I set off in the J4. It's narrow lanes all the way, and halfway there I saw lights coming through the darkness. I pulled in and waited for them to pass. I didn't know who it was, but they recognised the vehicle. They must have seen the glasses shining because as they passed they shouted, 'Goodnight Mrs Harris.' My heart was in my mouth. I drove on carefully and met Mother and Father, who were very surprised to find me sitting behind the wheel. Father was full of praise.

BOMB

One Saturday afternoon Peter Smith from Bowden's turned up with a Land Rover full of scrap. He had been clearing out his back yard and sorting out the shed behind his shop in Chagford. Father and I were there to help unload, and Peter was in the back of his Land Rover throwing off the scrap at the bottom entrance to the yard. We sorted scrap as we went, throwing light iron on the light iron heap, heavy iron on the steel heap, with Father picking out the non-ferrous metal to take up to the workbench.

Things were being thrown in different directions. All of a sudden Peter said, 'Catch!' He tossed a lump of iron my way and I caught it. I wasn't really looking; all I saw was a lump of iron, which I made to throw on the steel heap. Then he shouted, 'Don't throw that – it's a bomb!'

'A what?'

'It's a shell, a World War II shell!'

I looked down and saw it was a rusty old shell, about a foot long, with a brass point and detonator. It hadn't been fired and was still live!

I said, 'Fancy throwing it at me – I might have dropped it!' He just laughed. 'You wouldn't be laughing if it had gone off!' Father said, 'Take it up home.'

I walked up home with it and asked Mother where I should put it. She said, 'Ask your father.' So I put it by the front door and went back to unload the scrap.

No one thought any more about it. It stayed on the doorstep for weeks, until Mother couldn't stick it any longer. She was saying, 'Someone could drop something on it and it could go off. Someone is going to get hurt.' She decided it had to go, so she put it in one of her shopping bags and took it into Moretonhampstead police station.

She went in and placed her bag on the counter. The policeman on duty asked her what he could do to help her. She said, 'Could you take this bomb I've got in my bag and get rid of it for me? I'm afraid it might go off, or someone might drop something on it at home and set it off.'

The policeman said in a panicked voice, 'A bomb! What did you bring it in here for? It might go off in here!' 'I don't think so,' said Mother. 'It's been on the doorstep for weeks. I brought it in as

Sam hasn't got round to getting rid of it, he usually puts them in the hedge.'

'In the hedge?'' said the policeman. 'Yes, that's what he usually does.'

The policeman couldn't believe it. He came over to find the ones in the hedge, and got the bomb squad to come and take them away.

SHOOK THE HOUSE

As teenagers do, my brother Jim and his mate Rob had a thing about making explosives. They pinched Father's copper pipe (which he wasn't too pleased about) and made a mix of weedkiller and sugar, which they put into a short piece of pipe along with two bare wires, then pinched the ends tight. Then they'd place it in an old aerial pole, blocking the end with a lump of soil. They'd hold it on their shoulder and aim it at a target. If you touched the bare wires to a battery it would fire just like a mortar.

Later they had the idea to make a bigger one. They had a two-inch diameter copper pipe, about 18 inches long, which they filled with their mixture, then placed the wires inside. They placed it inside an old 45-gallon resin drum, and ran a long piece of wire to where we were hiding, behind an old car. I remember Jim putting the wire onto the battery. There was an almighty bang; we looked over the car and saw the drum go up into the sky, a ball of flames. The ground shook; the explosion was so loud it hurt my ears. The drum came down in flames, its end missing.

We were all in shock when Mother appeared wanting to know what was going on. She was concerned but cross. She wanted to know what the explosion was as it had rattled the windows and she'd felt the ground shake. She demanded that we didn't do it again, as somebody would get hurt. She hadn't to worry because Jim and his mate had frightened themselves enough.

People in the area were talking about the explosion for the next couple of days; a farmer said that his barn roof had rattled, and he lived a mile-and-a-half away. It had even shaken the roof at my Nan's farm at Lingcombe. A few days later we found the end of the drum two fields away!

WHEN I BOUGHT MY FIRST MOTORBIKE

I worked hard for my bike. I picked up bits of metal around the cars, like brass trim, wire loom, aluminium number plates and door handles, to save and sell. It took me all summer to get enough.

I bought a moped off my Father. It was a Honda pedal cycle and it looked like a push-bike with an engine. It needed to be MOT'd, so Mother took it to Newton Abbot for me and I decided to trade it in for a Honda 50 trial bike. The bike man said I could pick it up in a week.

The following week I picked up my 'new' secondhand bike. It was red and white with 'spud' tyres, a real bike! We loaded it on the lorry and took it home. The next day I was going to ride it to Okehampton. I set off nice and early and got there with no problem, but on the way home it started to make funny noises. I had to call Mother out to Whiddon Down to pick me up. Later that week, when Mother was going to Newton Abbot with a load of scrap, I returned it to the bike garage. The man said he would sort it, and to pick the bike up in a week.

A week later I caught a lift down on the skip lorry again and arrived at the bike shop. The man said he hadn't finished working on the bike. I would have to catch the bus home, so I ran to the bus station but found the last bus had gone. So I went back to the bike shop. I told the man that as he had told me the bike would be ready but it wasn't, and I had missed the bus and I wasn't walking 16 miles, was there any chance of a lift? One of his workmen was working on a big 1000cc motorbike. He said, 'I could give you a lift. I need to give this a run.' I thought 'Great!'

I waited half an hour and then we were off. He told me to hold on to the handrail at the back of the pillion seat. This was OK till we came to traffic lights. Every time we pulled away my bum would slide between my hands and it felt as if I was going to tip off the back. After the third traffic light I asked if I could hold on to him and he said that was OK.

The road from Newton Abbot is very bendy in places (and this was before the Bovey bypass was built). When we got out of Newton Abbot we were off at top speed. On the straight he was doing 100mph and down Bovey Straight he was doing 120mph! I daren't look as the cars and hedgerows were passing in one long blur. He had told me I had to relax and just go with him. This wasn't too bad but he kept up the speed on the bendy roads up to Moretonhampstead. He was leaning right into the bends and the speed was still up at 80mph. I was holding my breath: I was on the back of a madman and the edge of my boot was skimming the road as we went round the S-bends.

When we got home he asked if we had any spanners as we had come all the way with no brakes! I could have hit him, and called him a mad bastard. I was as white as paper, trying not to show him that he had frightened me.

This was the first time that I had ridden pillion.

Rabbiting on a Motorbike

I found when I rode my motorbike home through the dark country lanes I would see rabbits. They would sit up, dazzled in my headlamp, and only ran off when I got up close. A couple ran into my front wheel. I don't like eating rabbit but my Father loved it. I picked up a few that had been killed by passing cars, but I decided that I would have a go at killing a rabbit myself. I would catch a rabbit in my headlamp and as I drove closer I would speed up and kick the rabbit in the back of the head; I caught a few this way.

One night I was heading home and someone had knocked down a hare. I picked it up; it was still warm and supple, only just dead. So I hung it over my petrol tank, like I did with the rabbits, but the hare was very long and hung down both sides to my knees. It was very late when I arrived home, and Father had gone to bed. I called to him that I had picked up a hare. He told me to hang it up and that he'd skin it in the morning. So I hung it up outside the back door and went to bed. In the morning Father called into me: 'Where's that hare?' 'Outside the back door, hung up.' It was so long that the bloomin' dog had got it and ate it.

Mini

When I was 18 me and Sam picked up some scrap from a house near South Zeal. We noticed a white Mini Clubman sat in the drive. The owner had died and the family was tidying up the property to sell. They asked Sam if he knew of anyone who would like to buy the Mini. I gave Father a tug on his arm: 'I would like it, but you'd have to pay for it and I'll pay you back later.' Anyway they struck a deal and I had a Mini. Sam drove it home.

About two weeks later Father asked me to take him to see some scrap at Drewsteignton, but first to go to Chagford to pick up his pension. It had been raining for several days but this day it was dry. We headed out of Chagford towards Drewsteignton. When we got to the bottom of Chagford Father said we would go Rushford way. I told him it would be flooded. 'No, it be alright,' he said.

We went down the hill over the bridge. I could see the road was covered with water from my side of the bend. I said to Father, 'I'll have to turn around.' 'No, you'll be alright, it's not that deep.' I hesitated. 'Go on,' he urged.

We entered the water. As he had said it wasn't very deep, but as we went on around the bend it got deeper and deeper. It was a sea of brown water. Father said, 'Don't stop, keep going.' As I turned to look at him I could see the water was up level with the window. We were pushing through, making large waves up the hedge. The water by now was up level with the headlights. All Father kept saying was, 'Don't stop, keep going.'

We got through without breaking down and carried on to Drewsteignton. We arrived at the customer's place; the engine was missing and spluttering, like driving with kangaroo petrol. The customer made a comment about my car. Sam said, 'She only tried to drown me down at Rushford, I thought the water was gonna come in through the windows.'

'Cor Sam, it's been deep down there.'

Once I had dried the distributor cap and leads in the oven, the car was fine.

DONKEY JACK

Donkey Jack arrived in the back of an A60 van when I was about five-and-a-half years old. Dad bought him from the gypsies. My brother had wanted a black-and-white donkey for his birthday, but when it arrived six months later, at Easter, he wasn't that interested. I remember it well; the donkey was put into the garden overnight.

The next morning I asked if I could take him out for some grass. The answer was yes; but I was five-and-a-half, the donkey an 18-month-old stallion! I walked him up the road so he could graze the hedgerow. Time went by while I waited for him to eat, so I sat down because my legs were tired.

All of a sudden Donkey Jack mounted me, pushing me to the ground, biting me all over and pulling my hair out. I was squashed flat. I remember screaming my head off and kicking him in the belly with my heels. All I could see was his grey belly and his white nose, grabbing at my clothes. Suddenly he got up and ran one way and I ran the other, still screaming.

The donkey disappeared for some time. Then I found out he'd spent the 'some time' over on my Nan's farm. He had a visit from the vet. My cousin Kirsty and I used to go to see him out in the field. One day Jack put his ears flat back and frightened her so she started to run home. He took off after her with his neck out straight, his ears back, teeth bared, and gave one quick snap. She screamed and he ran off. She was left with a hole through her petticoat, skirt and pants. I bet she still has a scar to this day.

DONKEY JACK LOOSE IN THE FIELD

It didn't matter whether it was me or my brothers: if we went and caught Donkey Jack in the field without a halter or a bridle and jumped on his back he would give you the ride of your life. He would try anything to get you off; he would wipe you against the hedge, under the brambles or under the lean-to shed, which was just high enough for him to stand under to shelter from the rain. It would catch you waist-high, and you'd have to bail out as that would hurt. Bob said when he jumped on Donkey Jack the bugger would take off, bucking like hell and head down. His neck was like a slide and Bob would slip down to his ears. Then he'd lift his

Peggy and Donkey Jack, Yardworthy Pony Drift, 1981 © *Chris Chapman* head, so Bob's toes were just touching the ground, and he would still be motoring towards the hedge. Bob said, 'The bugger knew what he was doing.'

A DONKEY IN THE SCRAPYARD

Jack lived at the bottom of scrapyard but he was always breaking out. He often got in amongst the cars, where the grass had grown really long. To get there he would have to squeeze between wings and bumpers. Some gaps were less than 18 inches wide, but he would squeeze through. After he had eaten all the grass, he would blow up and couldn't get out, as his belly wouldn't fit back through the gap. He would have to stay there for 24 hours until he'd digested everything.

The customers would often remark, 'Do you know there's a donkey stuck in the middle of the scrapyard?' They couldn't see how he got there or how he would get out without being airlifted. Father would often say, 'I'll have to call the RAF then.'

DRIVING DONKEY JACK

Bob and I broke Donkey Jack to drive. Bob made him a four-wheeled cart from an old hand cart, which had a turntable. He attached shafts to it and we used to play in it and take dung from the dung heap out to the fields.

I had a two-wheeled cart made for him but it was too heavy, so I made one of my own out of some iron wheels from an old water butt and the remains of Johnny Arden's scurry cart. He would also pull an old Morris 1000 car bonnet, upside down. It was good for dragging out car engines for customers, and it was fun in the snow.

RIDING DONKEY JACK

Soon Donkey Jack was more mine than Bob's and I began riding him regularly. I often rode a circular route round the little by-roads near the scrapyard. I used to go down the rough cart track overhung with hazel, ash and elder trees. The track was often full of puddles made black by stuff from the scrapyard, which reflected the sky like mirrors. The brook at the bottom of the track had large stepping-stones to the right and a narrow clapper bridge on the left. We would go over the low footbridge, as Donkey Jack didn't like to walk through the river. We'd go to the end of the track to Jurston, a community of two farms and a house on the green on the edge of the moor. We would turn right and ride along the road over Jurston Bridge and I'd lean over the parapet from Jack's back to see the fish in the brook. I always wanted to try to 'tickle' the trout there.

Then the ride took us right at Yelland Lane, a steep farm track that leads up to Meldon Common. In our direction was another common called Stiniel Down. At the bottom of the down the lane crosses the brook and runs up the hill on the other side. Our little brook is the upper reaches of the River Teign which flows down to Steps Bridge and beyond. The next right turn in the road leads to the hamlet of Lettaford. Lettaford used to have a chapel and three farms, which were once working farms but are now holiday homes. Even the little chapel is a holiday home. The road ends here but I could carry on up the track through the buildings, around the back of the farm, down the lane past old Fred's place and back to Jack's field and home. Sometimes I would do the route in the opposite direction, but the whole ride would be about two miles.

DONKEY JACK'S BAD HABITS

Riding Donkey Jack was not the easiest thing to do as I used to ride him bareback. We could not afford a saddle and it would have been difficult to find one to fit him.

Sitting on Jack was like being perched on a greased pole, and if that wasn't bad enough he had a bad habit. If he ever spotted any poo – cow, sheep, pony, horse or even dog – on the road he would have to stop and sniff every bit! His head would go down and he was off like a hoover, inhaling its smell. At this point I would have no control; the more I pulled the more I would slip forwards, like sitting on a slide. After passing his shoulder there was no way back and I would slide down over his ears. Even standing on the ground I couldn't pull his head up. It would be fixed in the sniffing position until he had finished.

DONKEY JACK BIT ME AND I BIT HIM

I was eight going on nine. If there was a customer's wife sitting in a car waiting for her husband to take off parts or talking to my Father I often went and spoke to her with Donkey Jack. The wives would make a fuss of Jack, petting him through the window, but if they lit up a cigarette Donkey Jack would nearly get into the car as he would eat the cigarette if he got hold of it. The same if they had any sweets. Sometimes I would have to put my feet on the car door to haul his head out of the window.

Donkey Jack used to nip me sometimes. One evening he bit me quite hard on the inside of my leg and made me scream in pain. I was so cross because he had bitten me out of nastiness. I grabbed Jack's long furry ear and sank my teeth into the top of it. I was shaken with temper and still screaming. I must have hurt him as he groaned and started to bend down on his knees. My leg hurt for days but Donkey Jack never bit me again. He might have bitten someone else, but he never bit me.

GETTING DONKEY JACK TO JUMP

I was nine and I was learning to jump and play gymkhana games on the Ardens' ponies. I longed for a pony, but I had to make do with Donkey Jack. So in the evenings at home after school I made up a set of jumps to practise with. Donkey Jack watched from afar while I found poles, tyres and drums. I pulled old sideboards from between the cars that had come off old lorry bodies. This took me a couple of nights. I spent one evening painting everything with bits of old paint I had found on the baling pile. Donkey Jack would come and have a nosey around when I wasn't there; I knew because he got paint on his nose.

Donkey Jack had never jumped fences before. He only jumped and swerved around puddles, usually leaving me on the floor. So now I was going to get him to jump a set of small jumps around his field, all about two feet high.

Donkey Jack wasn't like a pony: you didn't just squeeze with your heels and off you went into a trot. No, with Donkey Jack you had to kick and kick and he would do a jig, something that was uncomfortable to sit. I walked him round each and every jump to have a good look before attempting to jump them. I got on him and kicked him to go something faster than a walk and headed straight to the first jump, some tyres hanging on a pole. I could feel him slowing up so I shouted at him, 'Go on!'

He didn't knock the fence over but just stopped where he landed, with his head down. He did this with every jump and I would either land on his head or the ground. Some nights he would go round at a jiggy trot and jump every one, but some nights he would lie down.

How I longed for a pony.

Donkey Jack and Peggy *Courtesy Peggy Harris*

DONKEY RIDES

I used to take Donkey Jack up to the car park on the moor, about half an hour's walk from home. I would give rides to the kids who stopped for an ice cream or a family picnic, sometimes on holiday. I would lead them around the car park for 10p a ride. Some kids would have two or three rides and they would fish around in their packed lunches to find an apple or piece of bread or a Polo mint and feed them to Jack.

I had to be careful because if I wasn't looking Jack would pinch the kids' lollies. They would stand in front of him holding them at just the right height, and when I was busy sorting out which one was going to ride next, Jack's big lips would curl round the top of the lolly and it would be gone. With brother or sister ready to ride and mother or father busy taking family snaps, saying 'Smile darling!', you'd suddenly hear a wail: 'My lolly! He's got my lolly!'

There wasn't anything I could do. I told them they were stood too close and Jack thought they were offering him their lolly. A couple of times he bit some small child's finger while pinching their lolly. They would cry, 'But he bit me!' I would tell them, 'He does that when you put your fingers in his mouth!'

For some children Jack was the first donkey they had ever met or had ridden. Some of them didn't even know how to pat him and were fascinated by his big ears.

Sometimes we would spend all day up there, from about 11 o'clock till we left at about 6pm. I would spend my earnings at the ice-cream van. The ice-cream man made the most of us as I used to spend my money on beefburgers and lollies for Jack and bottles of lemonade. The holidaymakers would see Jack and pull in.

When it was slack for visitors, I would swap rides on Jack for ice cream. The ice-cream man wasn't very heavy and he would ride Jack around and give me beefburgers and bread rolls for Jack.

One of Jack's bad habits up at the car park was to go dive-bombing for fag-ends. He loved the dirty things. He would sometimes try to pinch the visitors' cigarettes while they were still smoking them!

GOING SHOPPING ON DONKEY JACK

I used to search through the cars in the scrapyard, turning up
the seats for loose change, lost by the former owners. You'd be
surprised how much I would find, sometimes sticky with sweets or
green with age; sometimes so old it was out of date. With selling
the petrol from the cars to be scrapped I would get enough to go
to Chagford to spend my savings.

Chagford is a busy little village, and on Saturdays they often
had jumble sales. I would give donkey rides, taking the kids
around the car park. I used to give the jumble sale people half of
what I raised, and the rest I would spend in the shop. I would buy
cream buns and sweets, but I always bought Jack a bag of pony
nuts from Bowden's. I used to tie him up outside the toilet, which
is housed in a building known as the Pepperpot in the Square. He
was happy because people and children would pet him and old
Jim Hines, the greengrocer, would give him a carrot or an apple.

It was three miles to Chagford but we would cut up through
Yelland Lane to Meldon and down to Meldon Hall. This way
was very steep, up and down, but was the shortest. Jack was very
slippery to ride as I rode him bareback (which was all right as long
as there wasn't any poo on the way!). His trot was a jig – not the
easiest to sit, but it was better than walking.

I would buy a bottle of lemonade or a can of Coke and share
it with him. I got to drink first, while he sniffed loudly at the
bottle, stretching his neck out and nudging it with his rubbery
velvety lips. When it was his turn he would drink it straight out of
the bottle, sucking like a baby.

This was all right but he expected me to share my sweets as
well. He would hoover at my pockets and I would have to give
him a hard-boiled sweet or Polo. It was no good on the way home
if I tried to take a sweet out and unwrap it. His ears were like
radar; his head came up, his ears would waggle and you couldn't
miss them. They were about ten inches long. Then he would cock
his head to one side, lips twitching, squeaking for a sweet. He
would almost turn his head right round, his eye rolling. He would
come to a complete standstill and wouldn't move until he got one. It
didn't matter if there were cars behind or if you kicked him to walk
on; he wouldn't move until I popped a sweet into his mouth.

Sometimes if I refused to give him one he would lie down with
me still on him. His legs would just fold and bend and he was

down. He could do this anywhere, in any mood that took him. His best trick was to lie out flat and hold his breath, and many people were fooled into thinking he was dead. One day a lady came up and said, 'You poor darling, your donkey's dead.' She tried to get me to let go of the reins but I knew if I did he would be up and off and then I would have to run after him. He was good at staying just out of reach. I persuaded him to come to life again!

Ready for Moretonhampstead Carnival, 1980 *Courtesy of Peggy Harris*

DONKEY JACK GOES TO CARNIVALS

When Bob and I were nine we entered Donkey Jack in Moretonhampstead Carnival; we went as Steptoe and Son. We drove Donkey Jack in a four-wheeled cart three miles to Moretonhampstead along the main road. We had bits of old scrap in the cart and Bob and I were dressed up. I remember shouting, 'Rag and bone, any old iron,' as Bob drove Donkey Jack around Moreton in the carnival procession. Jack didn't bat an eye. The streets were crowded, it was a long evening and getting dark, so we left Jack in Moreton overnight and went off to the fair. We picked him up the next morning and drove him home.

A few years later I entered as an old prospector. Donkey Jack carried an old billycan, pick and shovel, a bedroll and an old rifle, not forgetting an old sieve for the gold. I was dressed up with a grey beard and looked like an old miner. We won first prize. We went to

Chagford Carnival a few weeks later and did just as well. After the carnival had finished, I was walking back through Chagford and I met Jim Vickers, who was a huntsman. He had been drinking and he collared Donkey Jack, pinched a motorbike helmet off his friend and rode Jack into the Three Crowns for a drink! He had a pint and the landlady said, 'Get that donkey outta the pub before he shits on the floor.' Luckily Jack did hold onto it until he got outside.

The last time I was in Moreton Carnival was when I was nearly 14. I was too big for Donkey Jack by then but not too heavy, just long in the leg. We went as a US cavalry rider as my uncle had lent me an old US cavalry saddle.

DONKEY JACK AND THE HAZEL NUTS

Father was looking after Molly Croft's ponies when she sold her house and most of her land at Jurston. She kept a quarter of it and ran her herd of Dartmoor ponies on the land that ran from the river up to just behind our little field and along the river towards Stiniel Down. We let Donkey Jack run with the ponies and when I wanted him I would have to search over several fields, sometimes going right down over the steep field by the river. There were badger setts and hazel bushes down there. I remember one year – I must have been about 11 years old – the bushes were loaded with nuts. I spent hours there cracking open hazel nuts with my teeth. They tasted so good, but in the end I broke my tooth. Donkey Jack ate his nuts cases and all.

THE DAY DONKEY JACK MET THE HOUNDS

One day Donkey Jack and I were heading along to Jurston Bridge when I heard the hunt. I couldn't see it, but Jack's ears were up. I felt him quicken (something he didn't do very often). As I came up to Yelland Lane to turn right all the riders came down the lane and turned left. This made Jack very excited. He was very bouncy and alert. The whole road from Yelland Lane to Stiniel Down was full of hunt followers, from children on ponies to aristocratic ladies and gentlemen on hunters, with a few local farmers thrown in for good measure. The hounds were right in front.

With this Jack started to trumpet 'Yee-orr, yee-orr, yee-orr' and was off at full gallop, yee-orring like a foghorn. All the horses in the road parted just like the waves of the sea. Horses were shying and leaping up the hedge with the toffs holding on for grim death, trying to get some control. Most horses hate donkeys and many had never heard or seen anything like it. I had no control of him; the more I pulled him to stop, the more I just slid closer to his ears. If you ever go hunting you should never pass the master or the huntsman but I had no choice. I passed the lot!

I knew I would be in trouble when we stopped right in the middle of hounds, where Jack proceeded to shame me even more by biting them, then picking up and shaking them. I looked up guiltily and saw Bernard Parker, the huntsman, laughing so much he was crying. The riders were trying to sort themselves out and settle their horses down.

Liz Arden came through the mayhem. I used to ride her ponies at Stiniel. She was so cross with us that she was shouting. She ordered me to take the donkey away and get a pony to ride from her place. Shamefully I led Donkey Jack away and fetched a pony. I raced back to find the hunt and met it coming straight at me. The pony, which had never been hunting in its life, turned tail and took off. I gave it up as a bad job and went home.

DONKEY JACK GOES OUT ON LOAN

On the outskirts of Chagford at the bottom of Waye Hill lived a little girl called Sophie who loved ponies. Unfortunately she was very allergic to them, so she wasn't allowed to ride them. When she met Jack she fell in love with him but had no reaction, which was great. We used to visit them and she would ride him. Eventually they wanted to borrow him for her to ride in the holidays. They made a stable in the garden and asked someone for the use of their field and everything was ready. It was good for him, as he wasn't being used at the time. I was riding more and more at Johnny Arden's stables, and I was getting too long in the leg to ride Jack any more.

One Saturday Clare Arden rode up to Meldon Common and we had a race to the top. From the top of Meldon you can look down over Chagford and I could see Jack out in the field with some sheep. I could see he was up to no good. He was chasing the sheep about. I turned to Clare and said, 'He'll be home tonight.'

Late that evening the Ardens gave me a lift home. When I got out of the car I heard Jack. He was at the gate yee-orring at me. I went up to him and said, 'You're home then you old bugger!'

When I went in Mother said, 'Jack's home!' 'I know,' I said, 'I seen him chasing sheep this afternoon!' And he wasn't just chasing them: he was pulling their wool out and picking them up and shaking them!

While he'd been away the silly old fool was having fun with Sophie. She would take him in every morning and watch television on him and share her breakfast with him right there in the front room.

GETTING DONKEY JACK STUCK IN A SNOWDRIFT

In 1978 it snowed hard and Father wanted some hay taken up to the moor for our Dartmoor ponies which needed some fodder in the bad weather. We couldn't get out with any vehicle so I took three bales on the car bonnet with Jack. The quickest way would have been up to Lettaford and up through the green lane but I knew it was too steep for Jack with the three bales. There might have been snowdrifts too, so we went up to the main road and out onto the moor.

It took me hours. It was completely white; you just had to guess where the road was. The only signs of life were animal prints in the snow. We had to go over several little drifts and I had to help pull when the snow got deep. When we got to the cattle grid there was a drift right across it, but luckily the gate at the side could be opened towards us and we managed to pull through. When we got to the top of the hill the ponies weren't there but I spread the hay in the shelter of a stone wall and headed for home.

I decided to try the short route home, down the green lane to Lettaford. When I got to the gate into the lane it was blocked by a drift, right up to the top bar. We walked back along the wall to a field gate. My plan was to cut down across two fields and into the lane further down. This gate was padlocked so I lifted it off its hangings and headed down across the fields and came out halfway down the green lane. I looked down it and couldn't see any drifts so I decided to go that way.

When we got to the bend in the lane it was full of snow which had blown in through a field gate. It looked level but the lane sloped away under it and I didn't realise that the snow was at the top of the hedge further down. I left Jack and tested the snow, which was crisp on top and solid enough to bear my weight, so I went back for Jack. I thought, 'It's only a little way. He'll be alright to walk that short way.' We both walked briskly up and round the bend but then all of a sudden Jack stopped. I looked round to see why and saw his legs go straight through the snow like four pegs. There was a crunching noise and he was suddenly up to his belly. He looked very funny and I tried to pull on his bridle to get him to haul himself out, but it was no good. He was stuck.

I was worried and ran home to get Bob and a shovel and we headed back as quickly as we could. I was hoping he had got himself out but he was still there. Bob said, 'How did you get him up there?' From the lower side of the drift he was about ten feet in the air, level with the top of the hedge! We dug the poor chap out and took him home. He was all right, just a little cold and very hungry.

Peggy and Jack (right) *Courtesy of Peggy Harris*

No Man's Bitter

One year a film company made an advert at the Warren House Inn. They changed the look of the pub and called it 'No Man's Land' as they were advertising No Man's Bitter.

I decided to drive Donkey Jack up to the Warren to see what was going on. I drove him in his four-wheeled cart down to Jurston. I had to get through the river first as Jack always tried to get over the narrow clapper bridge. Then it's uphill all the way to the cattle grid, then it's still uphill to the main road and then along to the Warren, uphill and downhill all the way.

I could see lots of lorries and vans, people milling around, mainly the film crew. There were loads of beer glasses on the tables opposite the pub as they'd obviously spent a lot of time drinking beer. When they saw Donkey Jack they couldn't resist him; the young women came over to fuss him, followed by others. I told them Jack liked beer, because a young man had a pint glass in his hand and Donkey Jack was sniffing it out. He said, 'I haven't a bucket.' I said, 'Jack doesn't need a bucket, he will drink it out the glass like you!' So the young man gave half a glass of beer to Jack and shouted to his friends, 'Hey look, this donkey likes a beer!' So of course a whole row of glasses turned up, and one after another they gave Donkey Jack a drink. Jack was loving it; he'd worked hard pulling the cart all that way and needed a drink. They were passing comments to give to the film director that this donkey would make his film! Donkey Jack had several pints and I had to stop them giving him any more as we had to drive home.

Donkey Jack Bullies the Chickens

I used to bring my pony in at night in the winter as I hunted him, and I had to bring Donkey Jack in as well because if I didn't he wouldn't be in the field in the morning. When I went to bring them in I'd have to catch Donkey Jack first and let the pony follow. If I did it the other way round, leaving Jack to follow, he'd go the other way, running off up the lane like a mad thing. In order to catch him I would have to jump on the pony and charge after him.

Jack had his own stable but he couldn't see out over the stable door. I put a block on the inside so he could stand with his front feet on it so he could see out.

In the morning he would trumpet his head off and kick the galvanised wall. Father would feed his chickens not far from the stable. If I opened the door Donkey Jack would barge past me and scatter the chickens to pinch their corn; he would charge straight through them, ears flat back, nostrils curled up, mouth open, neck outstretched, biting chickens that were in the way. Making a high-pitched squeaking noise he would stand over the corn, tail swishing, feet stamping, walking around in a tight circle, hoovering it up. When he had finished bullying the chickens he would head out to the lane – and every single time he'd put his nose to the ground, walk a tight circle with legs bent, then go down for a roll. Then he'd get up and do it all again. This is when I would grab him and take him up to the field before he could charge off down the lane.

Donkeys At Chagford Show

I used to take Donkey Jack to Chagford Show to compete in the Donkey Derby. We won it several years running.

One summer when we had six donkeys I took three of them along: Donkey Jack, Monty and Maggie. Jack was black, with a white belly and nose. I let a young girl called Anna ride him this particular year. She lived across the fields, next door to my grandparents' farm, and she was very fond of Jack. Monty was a stallion, a black donkey with grey flecks. A young boy called Christopher Maude rode him, on a promise as his mother had picked the donkeys up for my Father. And I rode Maggie, a slightly older donkey, a dirty white colour and very docile.

We entered the race; there were six of us competing. Monty was first, Jack second and Maggie third. Afterwards Anna and I decided to enter the gymkhana games; we won several and got placed in others. This upset a lot of the parents, as many of the ponies wouldn't pass Donkey Jack; some just don't like donkeys in the same way they don't like pigs. The parents complained to the organisers, saying it wasn't fair that a donkey should be entered and that we should be disqualified.

Luckily for us the organisers thought it was a bad job that the ponies couldn't beat a couple of donkeys, so we were allowed to continue.

Donkey Jack and the Customers

Donkey Jack was always breaking out of his part of the scrapyard; squeezing under the fence and through the cars. Customers often said when they were busy taking off car parts they felt someone push into them.

We had a customer one afternoon who said he hadn't looked to see who it was as he was busy, with his head under a car bonnet. He would shout out, 'What you doing mate?' Donkey Jack would knock into him again. Irritated now the customer emerged from under the bonnet to confront the pusher and came face to face with Donkey Jack.

One customer said he was lying under a car taking off a prop shaft when someone kept walking over his legs. He was getting annoyed with this person who kept knocking into and standing on him. He had been swearing at whoever it was but couldn't understand why there was no reply. He came out from under the car, ready for a fight. As he emerged into the sunlight he met a big nose sniffing at him: of course it was Donkey Jack.

Another day a customer came storming up the yard and told Mother, 'That bleddy donkey bit my arse!' He said he had been busy taking a part off under the bonnet. He had seen Donkey Jack eating grass behind a couple of cars. While he was working the donkey had come round the car. He ignored him, even when Jack had pushed into him. He was bent right over the engine when all of a sudden Donkey Jack bit him.

In Conclusion

When I left the scrapyard in 1986 Donkey Jack was living at the Miniature Pony Centre in the parish of North Bovey, but unfortunately he disgraced himself (in the same way as he did with me when he first arrived!) and so he was sent home. When Sam became ill with cancer he decided to sell Donkey Jack and took him to market – it was the last one Sam ever went to – and Jack was sold at the age of 16. Sadly I wasn't around to stop it, but I do know that he wasn't sold for meat. Donkeys live to a ripe old age, and I would love to know if he's still around.

Ponies, Pigs and Peacocks

A Pony called Mark

When I was young I always wanted a pony. I would often ask Father if he would buy me one, but he used to say that I had Donkey Jack to ride and I rode enough ponies at the Ardens' stables.

One day he was out picking up some scrap from Morgan Giles, and he had a pony for sale. He was 12.2 hands and only just halter broken. Sam came home and said that he had bought me a pony. He said how big it was and that it was going to be 'cut' [castrated], and that Morgan Giles was bringing it over the following week.

Morgan Giles said that the pony was called Mark, that he hadn't been handled much and I would have to be as quiet as sugar to catch him. I was excited to be having my own pony at last. I was ten and couldn't wait for him to come home. Morgan Giles suggested that we kept him in for a bit and handled him till he settled down. He was home for a week and every time I went near him at first he was nervous, but after a bit he settled.

Father sent the pony over to the Ardens to be broken. He was ridden there to settle him down for a few days, and then I was lead around on him for a while. One evening Johnny said that he was good enough to ride home and for me to ride him on. He led me home and I untacked him and gave Johnny back the tack. He rode off and I was left with Mark but no saddle. Father expected me to ride Mark bareback. When we tried this Mark wasn't having anything to do with it and dragged Mother, who was trying to lead him, right off her feet. He then proceeded to throw me off in the middle of the track. I tried to ride him bareback several times, but he was having none of it.

Father said he would only buy me a saddle if I rode him, but this was getting impossible – and on top of everything I was getting nervous of him.

One day Mark broke out of his field and disappeared, but some farmer found him and put him in their field. Mark never came home. Father sold him and then would throw up how well the pony was going and winning prizes for his new owner.

Peggy and Nobby at Howton Hunter Trial, Moretonhampstead, 1979 *Courtesy of Peggy Harris*

He would tell me it could have been me. I tried to tell him that I could have ridden him with a saddle, but he would say, 'You say you can ride but you couldn't ride him.'

I think he liked to prove I couldn't do it, but I was only ten and trying to cope with a pony that was newly broken wasn't the easiest job.

STORM

Storm was a Dartmoor pony I had when I was 14. He was six years old and belonged to Pat Gibson who lived near Kestor Rock. She used to ride out hunting and that was where I got to know her. She told me that she had two ponies, pure Dartmoor, and she had started to break them both to ride. Now both had problems and she said she had hurt herself falling off them and she was too old to keep doing that.

I agreed to go and look at them and would take one to break in. When I got there both ponies were out in the field on the edge of the moor. She had told me that one pony bucked very violently and the other would take fright, bolt and run blind. I said I would take the one I could catch first. I went out to the field, one pony ran off and I caught the other. He was Storm, the one that bucked! Pat told me that he had bucked her off and she had cut her head open.

'Oh right!' I said. I wasn't filled with confidence.

I took Storm home and put him out in the field. It was a couple of days before I did anything with him. I decided to start from scratch by lungeing him. This is done on a long rope or reins with the pony moving round you in a circle. I started to lunge him from a walk to a trot, using voice commands like 'Walk on' and 'Trot on', on both reins (clockwise and anti-clockwise) for an hour each day.

I went on to putting the saddle on him and lungeing him in that. Then we did long reining, where you control the pony from behind with long reins coming back along his sides through the stirrups. He walks forward and you follow, using voice commands and steering him in different directions.

I did this for several days until he was used to it. My main worry was getting on his back; I thought the weight of the rider probably made him buck, so I decided to make a dummy rider. As we always picked up leftover jumble from the local sales I stuffed a very large pair of trousers with rags. I tied the bottoms so the stuffing wouldn't fall out, then tied the top as well.

Peter Hutchings at Yardworthy Pony Drift, 1980 © *Chris Chapman*

I tacked up Storm, and when I brought the stuffed trousers in he took one look at them and backed off and put himself in the corner. His eyes were nearly popping out of his head; his back was up and he stood there and just snorted. I left the disembodied legs on the floor and left him to get used to it as he obviously thought it was a monster. When he realised it wasn't going to move or hurt him he relaxed and I could continue with my plan. I lifted it very slowly, moved quietly towards him and very gently placed it on his back. I tied it to the saddle and left him in the stable to get used to the weight.

The next day I decided to put the saddle and legs on him in the field, where it was safer. The stable was enclosed with scrap and if he took fright there he could get hurt. He was happy just standing still, but moving was going to be something new.

I led him to the middle of the field to lunge him with the weight on his back. He was walking very stiffly forwards, his back up, his eye rolling – and as soon as I let his head go down it went and he started to buck and buck. I still had him on the lungeing rein and he went round and round, bucking and bucking. He kept this up for ten minutes and finally I managed to change the rein. Because this was different he started to buck again. He gave up eventually as he had tired himself out.

The next day he was the same, bucking like a mad thing. He kept this up for five days. I thought I was never going to be able to mount him. For another week I just did ground work, lungeing and long reining him with the heavy legs on his back until he didn't care any more.

One day my eldest brother and his friend Rob were watching me working with Storm, and Rob shouted, 'Aren't you going to ride that pony?'

I challenged him, 'You can if you want to!'

'All right,' he replied. I knew if I turned Storm in a circle with two reins and one touched his tail he would buck, so I did this with Rob and Jim watching. Storm didn't let me down. He went round bucking and bucking. When he stopped I turned to Rob and said, 'Can you ride that?' His chin was nearly on the floor. I told him to come tomorrow and he could have a go.

The next day they came up and watched. I said, 'Ready then Rob?'

'No. I've changed me mind!'

I said, 'Well I'll have to do it myself then. You two can come and hold his head.'

As they were strong lads I got them to hold each side of his head and told them if he tried to put his head down to pull it up, and if he tried to lift it high to pull it down.

I mounted him very gently and sat quietly in the saddle. I told the lads to lead him carefully around the field. Storm's back was up ready to buck me off. The lads could feel him trying to put his head down but he couldn't. We went round the field three times. I decided that would be enough for the first time. I asked the lads if they would do this again the next day and so we did.

I asked Johnny Arden if he would give me a lead from his horse and take me out for a ride. This went well and he led me out for several evenings.

Then one day I decided to mount Storm on my own. It was a bit scary as I couldn't predict when he was going to buck. I found he would be very uptight for the first five minutes. After weeks of being ridden he began to settle down, but he would try and throw you off if you got off out on a ride and then mounted again. I made a point of getting off and on during the rides until he got fed up with trying to buck me off.

His training then went really well. I taught him to jump and do gymkhana games, which he was good at. He was very quick and could turn on a sixpence. That first winter he went hunting and loved it. We went pony gathering and he was very good at that too. If you took off after a pony that broke away from the herd, he would turn at the same time as the pony you were chasing – and if you didn't hang on tight you would be out the side door.

We used to ride all over the moor. I would jump gorse bushes on him and small stone walls and in and out of the river. I used to keep our river clear of anything nasty as we weren't on mains and it was our drinking water. I would ride up the river looking for dead sheep in the water, and we'd pull them out with a rope. He didn't mind, but he didn't like it when we pulled the head off a rotten one. I suppose it was the smell!

He loved competing. We went to a hunter trial at the Ardens. We jumped a round and came second, then spent the rest of the day riding round picking up the score sheets. Then we entered Chagford Show and came second in the Dartmoor race and won prizes in other games.

STORM MOVES ON

I used to go shopping on Storm and tie him up in the market place in Chagford. On the way into the village I used to pass two little girls who were twins. I knew them and their mother. One twin was very bold and outgoing, and the other was shy. I knew they could ride as they had an old pony, which they shared. The bold one asked if she could have a ride on Storm. I said, 'Yes.' Then I told her I would have to lead her as no one smaller than me had ridden him. I led her down around Chagford Common.

One day when I had to help out at home these two little girls came to the scrapyard and asked if they could borrow Storm to go for a ride. I said, 'Yes' as I didn't want to disappoint them. They were only seven or eight and they had come three miles. So I tacked him up and they went for a ride. The next day they were back for another ride.

Then they asked if they could borrow him and take him home for the holidays. As I was too big for him by then and was going to have to sell him, I thought these two girls would be good for him. One girl was a strong rider and the other was quiet. As he was a purebred Dartmoor they could show him as well as jump with him, do gymkhana games and perhaps hunt.

After a few months their mother decided to buy him. They used to take him up the garden steps to their house and ride him up the hill to his field. He would still put in the odd buck. He usually bucked them off into the nettles by the field gate.

The girls went on and won a lot of showing classes and gymkhana games. They had a lot of fun on him and when they grew out of him he went on to be a first pony for their godparents' grandchildren. There he spent the rest of his life. His brother ended up in the pot, and if I hadn't taken Storm on he would have gone the same way.

Sam at Yardworthy Pony Drift, 1980 © *Chris Chapman*

ROUND UP

There was a lady down the lane at Jurston called Molly Croft. She used to breed Dartmoor ponies, but in her early years she was a vet. She sold her house and moved to Cullompton but still kept her land. Father agreed to feed and look after the ponies through the winter in return for all the foals that were born. In a few years he had accumulated a little herd.

He used to run them on the moor through the year. October time the farmers would gather all the ponies in for the market. It was very well organised; we would be on horseback, driving them together in a big herd. Everyone would split up and scower through the bracken, hollering and whooping, some cracking whips. The ground was rough; rocks and ridges lay hidden underneath the heather and bracken. We would chase them in and out of rivers, round gorse bushes, down through one valley and up the other side.

The group would get bigger as the day went on, manes bobbing, tails flowing, heads outstretched as they bounded over the moor. Every now and then a stray one would make a break, turning back towards the area that they were familiar with. Once when a pony broke away from the herd I shot off after it on my Dartmoor pony Storm. We were galloping side by side, the other pony bounding over the furrows and tuffs within the land. All of a sudden it turned; but Storm was so quick he too practically turned 'on a sixpence'. I nearly fell out the side door, over his shoulder. The only thing that saved me was my heel getting caught under the seat of the saddle, and grabbing a handful of mane. I had to pull up and start again.

The drive would finish at Tawton Gate cattle grid. Ponies would be huffing and puffing with sweat-soaked necks, steam rising from their backs. Mares would be whinnying for their foals, and foals squealing for their mothers. Some would huddle together, pushing and shoving. Nostrils would be flaring, their breath coming out in big puffs, flashing the whites of their eyes.

It was only a few yards further down the road to Yardworthy, a Duchy of Cornwall farm. This is where the farmers would sort out their own herds and take them home. They would later be divided up into groups: the new foals that needed to be branded and the colts, old mares and other unwanted ponies to be sold.

They were later loaded into lorries and taken to market. The newly branded young fillies would be released back onto the moor with the other mares.

Once we got our ponies home we would put them in a yard, for a couple of days. The ones that were going back on the moor would be hot-branded with a letter 'H'. My brothers and I would drive them into a dark stone barn, where it was easier to catch them as they had less space to run. It was known as 'The Wall of Death'. You had to grab a pony around the neck, the other hand would grab onto its head. Off you'd go, bouncing off the walls, bouncing off the other ponies, getting pushed into the back of them. They would turn their backs on you and rump up, likely to kick out at you. It was dark and you could hardly see. The only light came through slit windows in the stone walls.

Father would have a fire outside, heating his branding iron till it was cherry red. The door would swing open. All you could see was his silhouette filling the doorway. In his hand he'd be clutching onto the iron. 'Hold 'em, hold 'em', he would shout in his deep Devon tone.

Off you'd go again. The ponies were startled and unsettled by his entry. Once we had the pony still, Father would lunge forwards to brand it on its left hindquarter. It would either run backwards or shoot forwards. I'd always be scared that he'd get my arse instead of the pony's. This would happen to each one before they were driven back up to the moor.

COLLECTING MAGGIE THATCHER

Early one spring Father bought a donkey from round the back of the Finch Foundry out at Sticklepath. He took me to pick her up; she was an elderly donkey, more white than grey. It must have been around five o'clock, and I had to ride her home. Father told me to get home before it got dark. I asked the lady what the donkey was called and was told 'Maggie Thatcher'. They had a good laugh.

I put on the bridle and jumped on her back, and trotted off down the road heading home. I had to go along the main road [the old A30]. We trotted all the way down to South Zeal and turned off on the back roads, past East Week and Gooseford and East Ash. We walked and trotted all the way, but she was getting tired (and it was getting darker). I had no sense of time, as I had no watch. We got to the top of Washford Hill and could see the road getting darker down the other side: the trees met overhead, and it was like going down a dark tunnel.

I could feel Maggie was wearing as she was taking smaller steps. Then from behind I heard a motorbike. The lights came around the corner and hit us and created a big shadow. Maggie froze; I couldn't get her to move. The motorbike rider stopped behind us, but poor Maggie was frightened of her own shadow. So I asked the rider if he would come alongside and light us down the hill. He agreed and we managed to get down and the biker went on his way.

When we got over to the hunt kennels it was very dark so I decided to leave her there and put her in the field. I hadn't seen my parents – who would have come the same way – and I hoped I hadn't missed them while I was putting Maggie in the field. I still had a good three miles to walk home and it was uphill all the way. When I was nearly halfway I heard a vehicle coming; it was laden as you could hear it pulling slowly up the steep hill. It was Mother and Father. They pulled up, I squeezed into the cab and we all went home. I picked up Maggie the next morning.

DONKEYS FROM HATHERLEIGH MOOR

Father had bought scrap and three donkeys from a little old lady on Hatherleigh Moor. She was selling her farm as her husband had died. The old farm was a little run down and too big for her to cope with. We had picked up several loads and Father had asked a lady called Sue Maude to fetch the donkeys with her Land Rover and horsebox. Mother and I and my two brothers went out to help load the donkeys and bring the scrap back.

When we arrived the old lady had the donkeys in her back yard. Sue backed her horsebox into the gateway and dropped the ramp. The donkeys stood having a good look, ears pricked. I asked the old lady what the donkey's names were. She said the stallion was called Monty, the mare was called Esmeralda and was in foal, and the yearling was called Little Bugger.

We drove the donkeys up the ramp; Esmeralda and Little Bugger went in. The stallion didn't, so we put a halter on him and tried to lead him, but he dug his heels in and wouldn't move. We managed to push and pull him to the ramp but that was as far as he would go. The old lady picked up her mop, which was leaning against the wall, and started to poke him but he still didn't move. She put the mop between his legs and said, 'I'll polish his balls for him, he'll go.' He went; he went backwards. Sue was pulling on his halter; Bob and Jim were on either side of him, holding hands around his rump, pulling and pushing on his shoulder, forwards. Mother and I were pushing on his rump and he was still going backwards. The old lady disappeared into her kitchen and appeared with something in her hand.

'Out the way, he'll go now!' she shouted. With his she put something up under his tail. Reaching for the mop she said, 'Go on boy,' and starting poking him again.

'What was that you put under his tail?' we asked. She replied, 'Ginger.' We couldn't do anything for laughing; we'd never met anyone with that method before. He did go in.

DRUNK PIGS

My father used to keep pigs, and at one time we had a sow with five half-grown youngsters in a galvanised shed about 15 yards from the back door of the house. One day I was left at home looking after the place while everyone else was working, clearing a farm that had been sold. They were working for a week loading iron scrap into skips.

I began to notice that amidst the peace of the countryside the pigs had started making a lot of noise. They were bashing and banging their feed trough about, rooting into the earth floor and knocking against the metal walls. All the time they were grunting, squealing and barking noisily. They seemed to be trying to get out, and I didn't want to have to deal with loose pigs in the scrapyard.

Father had already fed them so I couldn't feed them again to quiet them. I gave them a few household scraps but that wasn't enough for six pigs. Then I had a brainwave. There was a lot of homemade wine around the place, which we had picked up three years before from a house clearance out at Gidleigh Castle. This wine was years old and we had given some away to people who would drink it. I remember giving a bottle of rhubarb wine to Johnny Arden. He said it was wonderful stuff, went down like syrup but him and his wife couldn't stand up after. He said, 'That stuff was good-dangerous stuff!' We had gallons of it kicking around the place. I tipped a gallon of the wine into the pigs' feed trough and they loved it, sucking and slurping it up. I gave them another gallon or so and those pigs were so happy! They lay down and slept, and when I went in after an hour or so they were very quiet. I was worried; I thought I might have poisoned them. So I looked over the door and there was one sat up like a dog leaning against the wall, others were lolling against each other, making little soft grunting noises and 'Wee wee wee' sounds. I said to them, 'Happy, pigs?' There were a few grunts and one or two looked up. I swear they were smiling.

Father came home and fed them, then came in and said, 'They pigs are quiet.'

Next day Father was gone again and the pigs were out there banging and crashing, squealing and grunting. They were making a hell of a noise, worse than before, so I thought, 'Can't put up with this all day.' I gave them two gallons more of the wine and they were quiet again, singing softly in the shed.

Father came home, went to see to his pigs and when he came in he said, 'I do believe them pigs is pissed! I thought they was pissed last night!'

The third day I gave them more wine but Father said that night, 'You'll kill me pigs if you keep them in that state.'

I still think the pigs enjoyed their party though.

This wasn't the only time I got pigs drunk. When I was about 13 I had two pigs that kept breaking out of their pen. They would watch me mending the fence, then lean on it and break it before I could fix it properly. Father had picked up a lorry load of beer kegs for scrap and some of them were still full. I worked out how to tap them and get the beer into a bucket, and then fed it to the pigs. This worked nicely. They were staggering about, singing, and eventually put themselves to bed and I could get on with fixing the fence. The next day I needed to finish it off but the pigs were so hung over and bad tempered I daren't go in there without giving them some more beer to cheer them up.

OILY PIG

Father went drinking with Jim Dunning, who used to be a farmer; they would usually go down to the Sandy Park Inn, on the other side of Chagford, or up to the Tom Cobley Tavern at Spreyton. These two spent hours together. On one occasion Father bought a young white boar pig from Jim. I remember this pig; he was very tame and lived free in the scrapyard, and grew into a very large boar. During the hot weather he would wallow in the oily puddles to keep cool and came out shining black as if he had been painted with black gloss paint. The only problem was when he was in this state he was rather itchy, and would try to rub up against you or the customers. Imagine it, the customers would run when they saw the shiny black pig grunting and trotting straight towards them! When he was in this state he would frighten people's horses riding by the yard. Horses are frightened of pigs anyway – let alone a shiny black monster like ours.

Down the back there were loads of 45-gallon drums laid on the ground. The pig took a fancy to them, and treated these drums as if they were sows. Bob told me that Father had found someone with a sow and lent him to Jan Routley, a farmer from Postbridge. He came with his trailer to pick the boar up to take him to visit his sow. Jan had parked the trailer close to an old car and stood on the other side with a sheet of galvanise so they could load the pig up into the trailer. But the pig was having none of it, and he knocked Jan flying. When they tried again, Bob said, 'The pig lifted the car with his snout, but he couldn't go under it as he couldn't hold it up.'

SAM'S SUIT

When Sam died we were asked what we wanted him to be buried in. We all sat in silence for a moment. He'd had a suit made by a man out at Postbridge, and it cost him £300. We all felt he'd paid too much for it. When he went out in his suit he'd wear wellie boots (see photograph opposite). I don't know why: perhaps he couldn't find his shoes. So I suggested his suit, as he'd paid so much for it! He might as well be buried in it to get his money's worth.

Sam and Jim Dunning at the Tom Cobley Tavern, Spreyton, about 1988 *James Tilly*

LITTLE PIGS

Father was cutting up scrap on a farm and noticed a little pig running about. He said to the farmer, 'That's a pretty little pig.' The farmer said, 'You can have that pig Sam.' Father finished cutting and loaded up. He saw the little pig go under the field gate and thought to himself, 'I'll catch it later.' When he was nearly finished he saw a buzzard fly up; he went out to the field to catch the little pig and found the buzzard had killed it. That was the end of his little pig.

Another time a farmer gave him a little pig that was the runt. He took it home and fed it milk and meal and bread. It was very small, but a pretty little pig. But it just shrunk; it never grew and it looked like a concertina, wrinkly in the middle with big ears and a long tail. The poor thing died.

BOSS

Father came home one night loaded with scrap and a very pregnant spaniel dog. She was about to drop, any day. It wasn't long before she had six puppies, all black and white, spaniel cross collie. When they were old enough they were snapped up by visiting customers, apart from one smooth-haired male which we called Boss.

We used to play with him, but one day when we came home from school he was gone. Someone had taken a fancy to him. Six months passed, then one day we came home and there was Boss. He was back; his owners couldn't cope with him. When they went to work they had locked him in the bathroom and he'd scratched off the paint and wallpaper; when he was in the garden he dug holes, so they brought him back.

My eldest brother Jim was fond of Boss and claimed him as his dog. Boss went nearly everywhere with Jim. Jim left earlier for school than us and used to walk up the lane, change into his shoes and leave his wellies in an old shed at Lettaford. Boss would walk out to the main the road to wait for the minibus with him, then find his own way home. But when Jim came home on the first day that Boss went too he put his hand through the broken door to get his wellies and heard a growl, which made him stop still. He said quietly, 'Boss?' and out came the dog; he had sat with Jim's wellies all day. Boss used to walk us all to the bus when we went to the senior school; at a quarter to five he would come and meet us.

We used to go rabbiting with him, with a car headlight and a battery. Father and I would spot the rabbit in the bright light and let Boss go, and off he would run. He would nearly catch it, turning it into the light, dazzling himself and losing the rabbit; he never caught many. Father would say, 'Nearly boy' and Boss would look up, tongue hanging out, panting hard, eyes shining like he was almost smiling.

Father often took him out in the lorry, and on the way home at night would let him out of the cab window if he saw a rabbit in the headlights. One night we had been out to a farm down very narrow windy, hilly roads. Father was a very slow driver and as we came round a corner there was a large rabbit. Boss spotted it through the window. Father told me to let him out, as we had a steep hill to climb. Boss was gone out of sight. Father started off in bottom gear, the engine of his laden Austin J4 growling. We crawled to the corner round which Bob had disappeared, and the next thing we saw was the rabbit coming back along the middle of the road. It shot right under the pick-up with Boss not far behind, running flat out. He came round the corner like a greyhound and, dazzled by the headlights, ran headfirst into the bumper. What a bang! Father braked hard; the rabbit was gone and poor Boss was howling. I opened the door and called him, and he jumped into the cab. He had a bump for a few days but wasn't put off rabbits.

Boss would sometimes wander off at night looking for a bitch on heat. He went off once and got himself shot. He had come home and lain down in a van where he used to sleep, and in the evening he came indoors to lie in my bedroom doorway. I bent down to pat him on the head and rub his back, and noticed he was bloody. I called to Mother, and everyone appeared; Jim carried him into the lorry cab and Mother and him took him to the vet. They had to operate straight away. The shot had gone through his spleen and the bullet was just under the skin, but Boss never woke up from the anaesthetic. It was a shame – he was a lovely dog.

LUCY

One summer Tom Broadway and his wife turned up. They used
to keep greyhounds to race, and they had a very shy greyhound in
the back of the van. They asked Sam if he wanted a greyhound,
as it would be good for rabbiting. Father didn't want the dog,
but when they told him they were going to have her put down
he changed his mind. She had been used for racing but she just
wasn't fast enough. She was a white bitch with grey and brown
patches, and was very shy and gentle. She was so shy she wouldn't
eat for a couple of days, and I remember feeding her by hand.
I used to let her off in the field for a run. There were wheel ruts
running across into the next field, and she'd run and bound and
jump the ruts until she'd had enough.

One evening she was running backwards and forwards
jumping the ruts when she let out a yelp and ran off home on
three legs. I chased after her, and caught her at the top of the
lane. Father was talking to a customer. He came over to Lucy and
me and said, 'It looks like she's broken her leg.' We went down
home, Father got a chopper and split some wood and ripped up
some bits of cloth into strips. I wondered what he was doing.
Then he said he was going to put her leg into a splint and she
would be as right as rain in a few weeks. And she was.

TYKE

Over the years Lucy had several litters of puppies. We kept one, a
black-and-white lurcher named Tyke. He often went out and ran
round and round the field. Once Mother took a whirly gig washing
line and stood it out there. Poor Tyke was charging around one
day; he hadn't seen the thin washing pole and ran straight into it,
head first. I was stood in the field watching him. It made him howl,
and he looked at me as if it was my fault. He jumped the hedge
and went back to his kennel and put himself to bed. He sat there
whimpering; I rubbed his head when I put his chain on. He was
back out barking again at passers-by within five minutes.

He was a good guard dog, and he'd bark at everyone. He
would wind Father up; Father would go across the yard to his own
caravan to bed. He would say goodnight and Tyke would come
out of his kennel and bark at him. Father would tell him to 'Get in
and lie down.' You could hear Tyke's chain rattle as he went into

his kennel. He would turn round and poke his head out and give a loud woof. Father would shout, 'Get in', then Tyke'd give another woof – but a little quieter this time. You could hear by Father's tone he was annoyed; he would swear and shout again, 'Get in and lie down!' It was as if Tyke wanted the last word. He'd let out a very quiet woof. You'd hear Father grumble as he got closer to the caravan 'Bloody dog!' Tyke would do this most nights.

My Goat

Our family often kept goats, which we would milk and breed kids from. Mother used to make junket, which I hated. The kids were usually sold on, but if we kept them they loved to run and jump over the cars – and they didn't mind if they were customers' cars. Even if there were people sitting inside they still did it. They would rear up and head butt each other, while the odd accident would spray a shower of currants over the car.

When I ran out of grazing I would tether them on the green up at Lettaford. I'd take them up there and back again in the back of an old Triumph Herald. Sometimes one wouldn't get in, but if I drove off without her she would have to run home after us, bleating all the way.

After I sold them people would still offer us goats. One day a lady turned up and asked if I had lost one. I said, 'No, why?' She said that there was a goat at the cattle grid at Jurston Gate, so I walked up and there he was. He was on the moor side of the grid, bleating and trying to get back across. Someone must have dumped him, and I knew he could not survive on his own: surprisingly goats cannot cope with extreme weather. He was a castrated white Saanen billy. I took him home and rang all the people I knew who might have lost him. No one claimed him, and the police said if no one came forward he was mine and so I got to keep him.

John Arden dropped by and said, 'You ought to break that goat to drive!' I laughed as I thought he was joking, but Johnny was an experienced horseman and broke horses to drive for a living. He said he would give me an old goat harness, and he fished out a green canvas set with bells around the breast collar.

I broke him to drive just like Johnny would a horse. This was fun and I started by putting the harness on him and letting him get used to it. He didn't mind and often his head would be stuck in the hedge eating, quite oblivious.

Eventually he would pull a set of pram wheels and he didn't mind what I did with him. People would stare, astonished, and would often make comments. He was so friendly he would follow me around like a dog and would come when I called him. But he didn't like it when farmers came to the yard; they would ask what sex he was and when I replied 'A boy' they would have a grope to see if he was entire. He hated this (and so did I, as when they groped him he would leap forwards and knock me over).

I kept him up at Lettaford, in a barn with a yard and paddock, and I would teach him every night when I came home from school. I really looked forward to my goat training, and by the time I'd had him six months he was pulling the pram wheels nicely.

One day when I came home from school he was gone. I looked everywhere and couldn't find him. I asked Mother if she had seen Billy. 'Yes,' she said, 'I sold him', and she opened her purse and gave me £2.50. I was upset that she had sold him, and even more upset that she sold him for a measly £2.50. I stamped the ground and said that he was my goat and she had no right to sell him. She just said, 'Well, he's gone.'

It wasn't until I was 21 and talking to my Aunty Angel about the goat that she said, 'Mother didn't sell the goat; she had me take him to the abattoir and you ate him every Sunday for weeks.' I remember those 'roast lamb' dinners, which we really enjoyed when things were as tight as they were, but I felt really gutted. She had even had the nerve to feed him to me!

PEACOCKS

One day Father was clearing scrap from Waye Barton, a big house just outside Chagford. New people had moved in with horses and dogs. The property had been sold with peacocks running around, plus doves. Their dogs were chasing them and had already killed several, so the new owners decided that the peacocks – and doves – should go.

They asked Father if he wanted them or knew anyone who did, as they were free to a good home. Father never turned down a free gift and probably saw a deal in them. Mother and I were sent to catch them, but when we arrived it was dark and the birds had put themselves to bed in the rafters of the big barn. All you could see were their long tail feathers hanging down in the torchlight.

The only way up was by ladder, and then you had to walk along a beam about 18 inches wide above the one the birds were perching on. I had to walk to the middle of the beam, then reach down, grab a peacock by its legs and pull it off its perch. That really made it flap! The only light I had to see by was the torch Mother was shining up from below. If I turned her way it would dazzle me. When I had a peacock by the legs and it started to flap it would make me wobble. I had to wrap its wings in quick, hold it close and make my way back along the beam.

We couldn't get boxes big enough to put them in so we used hessian sacks to carry them. I had to repeat this balancing act seven times! Then I had to box up the doves that were roosting up under the roof and on the windowsill. They told us to keep the doves shut in for several weeks before letting them fly because otherwise they would fly home.

We kept the peacocks in for a week and then Father sold a pair to one person and a single male to someone else, so we were left with four. These four lived around the yard. They were always showing off with their tails over their heads and squawking 'pea hark, pea hark'. You would hear them first thing in the morning when daylight broke. Being in a scrapyard, metal would heat up during the day and when it cooled it would make a sudden bang or a sharp ping and these noises would set the peacocks off: 'Pea hark, pea hark'. You could hear them for miles across the moor. They were silly birds and would get into fights with their reflections in mirrors that we had around the place from house clearances.

One bird ran away and we often saw him at the Miniature Pony Centre. We could never catch it though; it was off like a road runner as soon as it saw you. The other three decided to roost at Lettaford. We didn't mind as it was quieter without them, but our neighbour John Harvey would do his nut, saying, 'Them bleddy birds is scritchin' five o'clock in the morning!' So we had to go and round them up every evening and drive them home.

Customers at the scrapyard couldn't believe their eyes to see peacocks strutting around the place. Father would say, 'It's not just grand houses that have peacocks you know!'

As for the doves I let them out after about six weeks and they all flew out, did two or three circles around the yard, saw where they were, flew off and never returned. They had gone home to take their chances with the dogs.

OLLIE THE OWL

Jim was down in the woods playing with his mate Rob when they found a baby owl, a ball of fluff at the foot of a tree. It was squawking so he picked it up and brought it home. He fed the owl on cat food and bits of meat, and would pinch mice off the cats. It was a tawny owl, all fluffy with big round eyes and a large mouth, and it was always squawking. Eventually after a lot of feeding the fluff turned into feathers and Jim took to carrying the owl around on his shoulder. He nicknamed him Ollie.

Jim had to teach Ollie to fly. He would spend time tossing Ollie into the air, but he'd just flap down to the ground. Eventually Ollie learnt to use his wings and to fly. He took to flying around the yard, and one day he flew away. We assumed he went looking for a mate,

Jim and Ollie, 1985 © *Chris Chapman*

but then we found out that he'd flown to Manaton, several miles away. He had scared a few people because he would land on them, which they wouldn't expect! The sad thing was someone fed him bacon rind and that killed him, as birds can't take salt.

JACKDAW

In the spring of 1976 I got off the school minibus at Jurston with my brothers. They rushed off ahead of me up the track to get home first. The track crosses an open green, and on the right there is a house that sits on the hill. I noticed a young jackdaw hopping around on the grass by the track. I walked up to it but it squawked, hopped and flapped away. I noticed the house above the green had a bush with red berries growing on its garden wall. So I picked a few and tossed them to the jackdaw. It started to eat them and came closer, so I put out my hand and it climbed on.

I never knew the sex of the bird – I just assumed it was a male – so I walked home with the jackdaw on my arm. He flew up into a tree so I went inside and changed; I thought he would have flown away, but he was still there when I came out. The next day he appeared again after school. I would walk around with him on my shoulder. I would have to wear my hat down over my ears as otherwise he would peck at them and it would really hurt.

The jackdaw would disappear during the day and would only reappear when I came home from school. He did this for several weeks, and then he started to appear in the afternoons. We had workmen down in the yard baling light iron [to compact it]. George, one of the workmen, said, 'That jackdaw sits up in the tree squawking and watching us work, but when we light up a cigarette it swoops down and grabs it out of our mouths! It takes the cigarette up into the tree and sits with it in its beak, and after a bit tears it to pieces.' This would infuriate the workmen – especially if it was their last cigarette – and they often threatened to kill him.

Some customers liked him and others didn't. A family used to come to the scrapyard from Moretonhampstead and the father kept asking me to sell the jackdaw to him as his children would love to have him. So I sold him to them, as my Father would have done (and because the workmen might have killed him for stealing their cigarettes). My brothers often said I was wrong to sell him as he was a free bird, but he did have a good life in Moreton. He flew off one day.

JO CROW

One time Jim found a baby crow that had fallen out of its nest. It was the ugliest thing you'd ever seen: covered in stubs, no feathers, small beady eyes and a large sharp beak, and it croaked and squawked. Jim kept it in a cardboard box and fed it regularly. He called it Jo, so he was known as Jo Crow. He grew into a fully fledged crow, and Jim used to carry him around on his shoulder.

Jo Crow would fly around the place, amusing himself by picking up shiny objects and flying off with them. He usually put them in Sam's bed. So every night when Sam turned in he would have to empty it out. Jo Crow would place the pieces in the folds of the blanket, nuts and bolts, silver fag paper, bits of mirror, allsorts; he had the whole scrapyard to search! Sometimes you'd hear Jo kicking up a fuss and you'd find him on the workbench tugging at a very large shiny spanner.

One of his habits was to annoy Patsy, a Springer spaniel. Patsy was kept tied up as she would disappear hunting, and she liked to lie out across the path at the end of her chain. Jo Crow would hop along the path behind her and peck at her tail or feet. She would yelp and jump up and bark at him. Jo would flap away. Patsy would then lie down the same way and Jo would sneak up on her again. She never learnt to lie down the other way so he couldn't get her.

We used to have Muscovy ducks, a drake and two females. Jo Crow would fly over the top of the drake's head, just missing it, squawking as he went. This would frighten the drake, and he'd start strutting along hissing and huffing. It was fun for Jo Crow. One day Jo must have been annoying Patsy and couldn't have seen the drake coming. The drake pecked a big hole in his back and nearly killed him. Mother heard all the flapping and squawking and saved him, and treated his wounds with her homemade plantain ointment. Jo Crow was very sorry for himself for several days, and stayed in a box indoors until he was well enough to venture out. Then he was back to his old tricks, swooping on customers. You always knew where he was: he was very noisy, or you'd see him tugging at a bit of rubber and poking his beak under rubbish to get a bit of shiny metal. He would fly off with it and you knew where he was going: to fill Father's bed.

One day Jo Crow had been near the house all morning. We'd been sorting loads ready to go up the road, and the lorry and pick-up were ready to go. We all went in for a cup of tea. Jo Crow started squawking near the door, so Jim went over, put out his hand and lifted him up. Jo Crow just collapsed in his hands and died.

THE GUARD TURKEY

I was sent with a workman to pick up some scrap from Bowden Farm, near North Bovey. You had to go down a bit of a track to get to the place. I pulled up in the farmyard in a red pick-up truck. I got out and knocked on the front door, but there was no answer. When I turned back to the truck there was a very large turkey. Up until then I had never seen a fully grown turkey. This one was bronze; he was puffing up his feathers and strutting about making gobbling noises in front of the pick-up. I had to walk past him, but as I did so he charged and jumped and missed. I went to get into the pick-up but he was coming right at me again. So I ran around the back of the pick-up and he was on my heels.

I shouted to the workman who was sat inside to open the door. He replied, 'Not bloody likely!' and sat and laughed. In the end I jumped up over the tailboard. I thought the 'blimen' turkey was going to follow. As I got my breath back I cursed the workman for not opening the door. I could see the turkey's head popping over the sideboard and disappearing again, up and down. He'd made his mind up to get me. I had to climb through the driver's door window. I started up and turned round to go; back up the lane we met the farmer. He had a big grin on his face, and asked whether we had any trouble with the turkey as, 'He's a funny bugger, he attacks the postman every day. He only attacks when you knock at the front door.' I told him he'd chased me around the truck a few times. Farmer told me they had got him as a chick and they were going to fatten him for Christmas. Christmas came and the wife didn't want him to kill him, so they ended up keeping him as a pet. I would say more like a guard dog!

Scrapyard Characters

Newton on Saturday

Back in the early seventies Father always went to Newton Abbot on Saturday mornings with all his non-ferrous metals. Us kids nearly always went with him, in the pick-up or lorry. It would be loaded with copper tanks, bags of brass, batteries and so on. We'd sit in the cab and fight over who was going to sit on the seat or the engine. Father always filled up with petrol out at Beetor filling station before going, and we'd pick up some sweets for the journey. Father always liked to take the scenic route: down Long Lane to Manaton, past Becky Falls, out over the moor past the Bovey valley. Father never drove over 30mph so it was a long journey. Bumping along in the rattling vehicle, engine roaring, pulling its heavy load.

Eventually we would arrive at Newton Abbot. We would go round the clock tower and down a very narrow lane, a dead end. At the bottom was a little humpbacked footbridge over the river. There was a high wall all the way down on the left, and at the bottom on the right was a narrow lane that was full of lock-ups. The last three or four were Pearse's Metals. There were lots of other workshops further up. Father often sent us up through the lane to the main street to buy bread while he unloaded the metals.

There were always two men at Pearse's, Bill and Joe. Joe used to weigh the metals and Bill did the paying out. Joe always saved a cardboard box of toys for us. When it came to paying, Father would go into a very small office, with a desk. Bill would be sat in the corner on a square stone block. When it came to counting the money, he would get up, lift his cushion and take a metal lid off the block. Then he'd put his hand inside and pull out a bundle of money – that was his safe.

Indian Salesmen

Father would sometimes buy clothes from a couple of Indian travelling salesmen who called from time to time. Independent travelling salesmen were quite common in the countryside at that time and were useful for people living in isolated spots. The two Indian chaps always made us a chicken curry, which they cooked up in the back of their van. You could smell it all the way to the

Sam and Peggy, 1981 © *Chris Chapman*

bottom of the yard. When it was ready the old Indian chap would dish out a heck of a plateful of rice with curry piled high for Father. He would give us kids a smaller amount and a chapatti, which looked like the side of a saddle and we thought was like rubber to eat. The old man would say, 'Curry very hot!' and it was. It could blow your head off and sometimes I couldn't eat it.

Father and the salesman would drink whisky with their meal, and Father would have sweat running down his face. Mother didn't like curry and never ate it.

After the meal the suitcases of clothes would come out, mostly very brightly coloured Indian cotton. Father often bought shirts for himself and he sometimes bought things for us like jumpers. They were usually red, orange and yellow, which we thought were horrible.

GRIT DOWN THE CRACK

It always annoyed me when men used to come to the scrapyard for spare parts, and when they bent down their bums stuck out over the top of their trousers. It's what they call a builder's bum. When I was young I used to think it was very rude.

One day there was a plump chap in the lane just outside the yard, squatting down at a front wheel of an old Morris 1100, with his bum showing. A fag hung out of his mouth while he spoke to his mate. His greasy hands were slipping off the spanner while he struggled with the nuts on the wheel hub.

I ambled up to see if there were any new cars to rummage through and see if there were any 'goodies' or loose change. This was when I came across the plump chap. I decided to tell him to pull up his trousers as I was always told to pull up mine. He ignored me. This made me very cross; I was only eight at the time and I didn't like the look of his arse hanging out over the top of his trousers. I decided to make him pull them up, so I picked up a double handful of grit and poured it down the open crack.

Now this wasn't any ordinary grit – it's a mixture of fragmented glass from broken windscreens, black dirt from years of scrapyard rubbish, rust particles combined with normal grit. It was just like tipping dirt down a funnel. I jumped back as the man sprung up and spun round facing me. He didn't half move! He was up like a shot, dancing around. It wasn't until years later that I realised why he jumped round so much.

He chased me round the cars shouting, 'You little bugger!' but I was too quick for him, as every now and then he would have to stop and remove some grit. His mate was doubled up laughing.

HELPING A CUSTOMER

One Sunday I was playing around with Donkey Jack, driving him up and down the lane. I would ride on an upside-down Morris 1000 bonnet, like a sledge. As I went past the bottom entrance a customer came out and asked if he could borrow a wheelbarrow. He was a black man; I'd never seen a black man before. I asked him what he needed it for and he told me he was taking a gearbox out and it was too heavy to carry. I said I would pull it out with Donkey Jack, so we went into the scrapyard. He rolled the gearbox onto the Morris bonnet sledge and I led Jack up the lane to his VW camper van and helped him load it.

He was a man in his late forties, slightly greying. He gave me a fiver and thanked me. I was pleased; it was a lot of money to me as I was only ten years old. He told me that people didn't like to help him where he lived. I asked him where that was and he told me he lived in Plymouth and the people down there weren't as helpful as me. I asked him why and he said it was because he was black, I didn't understand. I told him I was blacker than him as I was covered in scrapyard dirt. This just made him laugh.

CHRIS, JANNY AND MATTY

One day when I was about ten Johnny Arden told me if I had somewhere to keep a pony I could ride one home from his place for the weekend. It would save him from dropping me home on a Saturday night, and if it worked out I could have a pony over the holidays. I knew Chris Hill up at Lettaford Farm, and I asked him if he would let me use one of his old stables. Chris was a retired farmer and his barns and stables were empty. He showed me a stable just beside the yard gate, and told me if I cleared it out and kept it clean I could use it as long as I liked. I was pleased. I got Bob to help me clean the old stable out.

We were wheelbarrowing out the dusty old dung when the upstairs window opened and Janny Leeman, Chris's brother-in-law, shouted, 'What you buggers up to?' I shouted up that Chris had said I could use the stable. He replied, 'You lying bugger,

bugger off! If you ain't gone by the time I get down, I'll give you an 'iding!' Of course we weren't hanging round. When I saw Chris he told me I was to take no notice, but I was too scared of Janny so I never used the stable.

However, Janny could be nice. He used to do a lot of the cooking. He grew potatoes in the garden and would sometimes give me a big red teddy, and I'd take it home and Father would fry it in round chips. We would share it. Janny was an old man; he used to wear britches with leather gaiters and hobnail boots, a shirt with no collar, a waistcoat with a pocket watch, black jacket and a trilby hat. When it was raining he wore a hessian sack over his shoulders. He had a very old black-and-white collie dog; you would see him dragging wood and faggots in over the green at Lettaford. Sometimes he would shout to you, 'Hey chil' come give a hand, I'll pay you.' So he would get you to help bring in the faggots that he'd chopped with his billhook and tied up with baling cord. After the job was done, he would take out his leather purse and find a 5p piece and say, 'There you go chil'.' It was like he was giving you a pound note.

Sometime after Janny had died I asked Chris if I could use the stable as I had a pony I wanted to break to ride. I only wanted to use it for a few weeks. I would see the pony three times a day. I told Chris's wife Matty that I had a pony and could she be quiet and not throw anything at the wall, as she had a bad habit of throwing buckets and pans when she was upset. Things were going well; I had managed to get a halter onto the pony and lead him out to graze. One day I turned up and the pony was in a sweat, his eyes popping out of his head. Matty had been throwing pans at the wall and wailing, and this had frightened the pony. It was no good – he was too wild to handle and I had to let him run free on the moor with Father's mares.

CHRIS HILL GOES TO THE PUB

Chris went to the pub every day for years. He drove a Morris 1100, and then he had a red Simca. He gave me a lift a couple of times. He was a steady driver, not very fast – which was just as well because he really wasn't fit to drive. He would drive straight down the middle of the road; he sat one side of the white line and I sat the other. He would only move over when he saw a car coming, then he would move straight back over the white line again.

THE CIDER JUG

In the early seventies a young man used to work for us and lived in a caravan in the scrapyard. He and Father used to go out to farms to cut up and pick up scrap. He'd been in trouble with the law and had spent time in Dartmoor Prison for theft, but Father always gave people a chance. His family was always in trouble. He went home at weekends and came back late Sunday night ready for Monday morning. Occasionally Father gave his Dad, Sid, a job. Father and son were often sent out on farms to pick up scrap.

Without my Father knowing they had decided to go back one night to pinch a generator from one of the farms. A few days later the police came to the scrapyard and asked if anyone had tried to sell us a generator, and they wanted to question our workman. Mother told the police officer that he had come back very late in the week and had unloaded something and put it behind his caravan. So the policeman went and had a look round and found the generator covered up. They arrested him and took him away for questioning.

A few nights later Sid turned up. He and my Father sat and drank cider all evening. Sid was telling us kids the story of how his son was arrested and how some bugger had grassed him up! We never knew that Mother had helped the police. We just thought that Sid was telling us a tale. Mother came into the room, from listening in the kitchen, and said 'Hadn't you better go home now, it's getting late.' She was looking very angry; she scowled at him for bad mouthing the police as she wanted us kids to grow up respecting the law. Father said, 'Now, now Mother!' and poured Sid another glass of cider out of the freshly filled jug. 'Drink up Sid.'

Mother was at boiling point: she wanted Sid to leave. Father had suggested that they intended to finish the whole jug of cider. So with that Mother picked up the jug, almost in slow motion. She poured it over Sid's head and said, 'He's had his cider, now leave!'

JOCK AND THE ANVIL

Father had been out to Mrs Stevenson's, the builders in Chagford, picking up scrap. Mrs Stevenson asked Father if he had ever come across an anvil as she would like one. It was a while before Father found one and took it down into Chagford with Jock, his workman. Father told Mrs Stevenson that the anvil was too heavy for him to lift off the lorry, but if she bet Jock he couldn't lift it he would prove her wrong. So Mrs Stevenson told Jock, 'You can't lift that, it's too heavy for you!'

Old Jock got hold of the anvil in his two arms. She said his face went bright red, it looked like he was going to blow a gasket – but he lifted the anvil off and placed it where she wanted it. She said Father was bent double laughing.

Jock (William Stuart-Porter) *Courtesy of Peggy Harris*

JOCK

Jock was a Scotsman; he had been in the army and had seen action in the war, but this had left him with a drink problem. I don't know how he got to know my Father, but he worked for Sam for years. He was left in charge of the scrapyard when Father was away. Father would never know what state Jock would be in when he got home; he could be laid out cold drunk or staggering. Father often played tricks on Jock.

One day Jock was laid out cold drunk. A little boy was in the scrapyard with his father taking off spare parts, when they noticed Jock. The boy asked Father, 'Is that man dead?' 'Yes boy,' said Father. 'I got to bury him in a minute.' The boy's father knew Sam was playing a trick as he could see that Jock was drunk. Father and the customer dug a shallow grave and laid Jock in it with his head stuck out the top. They carefully covered his body and left him there for the night.

Another time Father asked Jock to look after the place and told him not to get drunk. 'No, all right Sam, promise,' Jock chirped. 'I won't touch a drop, Sam.'

Father went out picking up scrap from nearby farms. When he came home he couldn't see Jock anywhere. Father's friend Taffy, a Welsh long-distance lorry driver, pulled in at the same time. Father told Taffy that he reckoned Jock was drunk somewhere around the yard. They found Jock, drunk in his caravan. He was making out that he had broken his leg.

'I broke me leg Sam,' he slurred 'Haven't touched a drop, can't move, broke me leg.' Father turned to Taffy. 'The bugger's been drinking again, I'll fix his leg,' he grinned.

Father broke an old gate up for the shimmers (the long cross pieces). He went down to the old cars and stripped out loads of flocking (stuffing from the seats), which looks like cotton wool. He also found some bandages. Sam and Taffy then headed back to Jock's caravan.

'It'll be alright Jock, Taffy knows first aid as he's a long-distance lorry driver. We'll fix your leg up,' my Father grinned.

They put one shimmer up under Jock's armpit, with another one on the inside of his leg, to make a split. They then packed the flocking round and wrapped it up with the bandages. His leg was as big as his own body. Father made a big jug of tea and added more than sugar. He sent it in with Taffy, who told Jock to drink it up as he thought it would do him good. They left him overnight.

The next morning there was a crashing and banging from Jock's caravan. Father looked out of his window and said all he could see was 'an enormous bandaged leg coming out of the door and Jock fell after it'. Poor chap couldn't make it to the toilet.

My Father sneaked off for the day as he couldn't face him. Late that night he found Jock sober and sat in Father's caravan with his chin resting on his hands, leaning on his walking stick, saying, 'You bastard, Sam Harris, you bastard!'

THE FARMER AT POSTBRIDGE

One day we had to pick up some scrap from a farm out at Postbridge. The chap was a rough farmer. He lived in a old farm on the moor but there were two houses at his place: one he lived in, the other was for the pigs. When you looked over the gate it was hard to tell which house he lived in.

We had loaded the lorry with scrap and the farmer asked us if we wanted a cup of tea. Father never said no to a cup of tea, and this was interesting because I didn't know which house we were going into. Having waded through the muddy yard we went into the one which looked like it was being used as a dog kennel. He used to breed wolfhounds, which were running in and out of the house. They were big gentle giants, hairy and friendly, but quite loud when you first arrived at the gate.

As we went in I saw a scrawny old cat, a bag of bones. Its eyes and nose were a mass of bubbling snot and it was licking the top of the milk bottle. The farmer poured the tea and asked if I wanted one. I said, 'No, thanks' pretty quickly. He turned to the table and said, 'Get out cat,' pushing the cat out of the way, then picked up the bottle and poured the milk in Father's tea. He passed the cup to him and sat down to drink his own.

Father was a short man with short legs and a big belly, and always rested his cup on his knee. The wolfhounds came in with no warning and one put his nose straight in Father's cup. With two or three laps it was gone, Father holding his cup in one hand and pushing the dog's head with the other, shouting, 'Get out of it, you bugger!' With this the farmer got up, pushed the dog away and took Father's cup. 'I'll get you another one, Sam.' He put the cup on the table and refilled it. He never washed it and handed it straight back to Father!

There were 14 wolfhounds roaming around his house. You just imagine the state of it, big brown steaming piles to step over. I think it would have been cleaner to have a cup of tea with the pigs!

FRED

Fred was a chap who lived at our place since before I was born. He was a Special Policeman one day a week, and lived in a caravan at the top of the scrapyard. Through the week he would pick up scrap metal from around the cars and clean it. This would mean separating the iron from other metal, and Father would pay him so much a pound. Fred was dirty, greasy and old. He would burn rubber in his fire for heat and to cook on. He was as black as a crow from the smoke, but on Saturdays he would clean up and go to Exeter to be a Special Policeman. His home was filthy from the dust and smoke too. At Christmastime he would buy us books, which he would wrap up in old newspapers tied with baler cord.

Although Mother hated Fred, she used to have him in for Sunday dinner. Because he used to look after pigs back in the sixties, he would come in covered in slime with the odd maggot on his shoulder from where he'd picked up a dead sheep from the moor and carried it home. He used to bring in dead sheep and boil them for the pigs. They fed anything and everything to pigs back then because everything was boiled first. The smell was unbelievable, worse than drains!

Mother couldn't stand it any more. He was banned from coming in. She still gave him Sunday dinner but he had to eat it in his own caravan. When it was ready she would shout for him. One day when I was fiveish he didn't come so I said I would carry it out to him. I got halfway along the path when I saw him coming. The tray was getting heavier and started to tilt, the plate started to slide and before he could get to me it was too late. The whole dinner – lamb, roast potatoes, peas and tinned carrots – was on the ground with the gravy running away into the scrapyard dirt. I was so upset because I knew there was no more dinner left to give him but he was so nice to me. He said, 'Don't worry, maid!' and bent down and picked it all up off the dirty ground. Bearing in mind it was a scrapyard – he took it off to his caravan and ate it.

FRED'S FOOD

After a few years he moved up the lane to a patch surrounded by
holly trees and built himself a house with sheds all around it. His
house was dug into the ground, four feet underground and five
feet above. His windows were level with the garden. The walls
were galvanised sheets reclaimed from the scrapyard. It was a very
dark, damp place with only a dirt floor, and he still burnt rubber
on his open fire. His sheds were full of old motorbikes and over
the years he collected cardboard boxes and gallon ice-cream tubs
that he would pick up from the ice-cream man who lived up the
road. He ate all the ice-cream leftovers from the tubs. Sometimes
there would be leftover sandwiches, out of date with green
mouldy spots and he would eat them as well, often offering us one!
We never accepted.

One year he spent the whole summer picking up faggots from
the neighbours' fields. He piled these on top of the roofs of his
sheds so his place was stuffed full. He had a little open fire with
a chimney crook to hang his kettle on over the flames. One day
Father offered him a half a pig's head. He said, 'Oh, lovely boy.
Proper!' He took the head and put it in a pan. A month later
Father had another pig's head and offered him another half. Fred
said he hadn't finished eating the last one!

Fred would eat anything. He had a lovely black cat and one
day I noticed that the cat had a burn on his back. Fred said he
had been scalded with hot water. Later, when I hadn't seen the
cat for a while I asked him, 'Where's yer cat?' 'I've eaten it!' was
Fred's reply – and he had!

FRED'S FIRE

Fred was 70, about the same age as Father, and when I was about
19 I used to take Fred shopping once a week as he was a little
frail. He was a very smelly passenger and six miles there and back
was a long way to suffer it. On one occasion he asked me to buy
him a small radio. The next job was to order him a mattress. This
arrived and he couldn't get it in the door so he cut it in half.

Later that day I called in to see if he was OK and he was sat
knee-deep in feathers. He was throwing handfuls of feathers at
a time into his open fire. There was a right smell and crackling
as they burnt. I said, 'You mind what you're about, you'll catch

yourself alight.' He said, 'No, I'll be alright, maid. It's only a few feathers.'

I left and about two hours later Mother was outside the front door when she heard this strange noise. Looking up the lane towards Fred's place, all she could see was a mass of flames. Fred's holly trees were ablaze and there was a great roaring, hissing, crackling sound.

She called to my Father who wasn't very quick, and Bob my brother who ran up to help Fred out. Fire engines from three towns were needed to put out the fire, and with the police there too there was no room for the ambulance to get down to pick him up. Fred was taken off suffering from smoke inhalation. Later the hospital tried to put him in an old people's home. He was having none of that so social services bought him a caravan and moved him back. He spent days going over all his burnt remains, sorting out what he was going to keep.

Late one morning he came down the lane hopping. He had a nail sticking out of his foot. Father sat him in an old car and pulled the nail out of the bottom of his boot. Then he took his boot off and gave me orders to get some water with disinfectant. We washed his foot, and Father kept saying to me, 'I think you should take him to hospital.' I told Fred that I was going to take him to hospital for someone to have a good look at his foot. The hospital was only three miles away in a Moretonhampstead on the edge of the moor.

As I was turning the truck Fred decided to walk to it, and walked straight through the black oily mud with his bare foot. We got him into the truck and rewashed his foot. In my mind I was thinking, 'Silly old bugger!'

Halfway to Moreton he started to groan and clutch his chest, and fell across the seat. I thought he was having a heart attack so I drove as fast as I could on the bendy road. I arrived at the hospital, rushed out, found a nurse and told her, 'I think he's having a heart attack!' The nurse knew him and said, 'Hello, alright Fred?' In a whimpering voice he said, 'No, I feel sick, she drives too fast.' The nurse said, 'He needs a wash up and he'll be back in a few days', and he was.

Fred was getting weaker every day. We couldn't look after him and I was taking him regularly to the hospital for his clean up. He had a daughter somewhere who helped him after the fire, but he didn't see her again after she found out that he had no money or property. The doctor decided that Fred couldn't look after himself and put him in the old people's home. He was never happy there.

When he lived near us the baker would come every Saturday. We always bought bread off him, and so did Fred. When he went into the old people's home Father cleared his caravan and he found, at the bottom of his bed, as hard as bricks, 14 green loaves of bread. Fred was tough as old boots and still managed to outlive my father by three years.

ODD JOBS

I did odd jobs once a week for Chris and Matty Hill, cutting sticks and splitting logs. Sometimes I took them waste wood from the house clearances. I would scythe grass and nettles and help in the garden, carrying buckets of water or pulling up old stalks of greens.

One day Chris asked me to give him a hand picking up stones from the garden. All I had to do was to fill the bucket with stones. This was an easy job, and as I threw each stone it hit the bucket with a clunk. Then all of a sudden there was a quiet 'stone'. When I looked down I had picked up one of Chris's poos! I couldn't believe it! I dropped the bucket and jumped over the hedge to the stream to wash off what I could, and ran home keeping my hand as far away from my nose as possible. I was urging! I ran in to Mother saying, 'I picked up Chris's poo! Quick wash my hand!' She was laughing because I was making such a fuss. She washed my hand with Jeyes Fluid and that really stinks too (but better than poo). I couldn't eat with me hand for a week and I refused to pick up stones any more!

NEWTON NUT

Newton Nut was a name we gave to a man who came from Newton Abbot. He used to come up to the scrapyard in the evenings to take spare parts off the old cars. I suppose he was a man in his late forties, with a large build. He drove an Austin A60, his car full to busting with tools, car parts and blankets. He used to sleep in his car a lot. When he came in the scrapyard you could hear him talking to himself while he was taking parts off, and this is how he got the nickname. He would be down in the yard for hours working in torchlight, sometimes until one in the morning. This would annoy Mother, because she would have to wait up. Sometimes he would ask for a cup of tea in the evenings. Mother spat about it, 'Bloody man, gonna be here late all night!'

One particular night, us kids told Mother we would make him a cup of tea, and we gave him a cup of tea to remember. We made a jug of tea and put Epsom salts in it with lots of sugar. He drunk it down and said it was a beautiful cup of tea. He carried on taking his parts off before heading home.

The next time Father saw him he never asked for a cup of tea. When Father offered him one he declined and said he'd had 'to stop in every gateway on the way home after the last time'!

TOMATOES

Most Saturdays a chap called Mr Harvey used to come to the scrapyard, always looking for a bargain. When we were very young he would bring us each an apple every time he came. Through the summer, without fail, he would bring a small crate full of different kinds and shapes of tomatoes. They were very nice.

I was about ten when I asked him if he grew the tomatoes himself. He'd brought us yellow tomatoes, and I'd never seen yellow ones before. He told me he'd got them from work. 'Where do you work?' He told me he worked down at the waterworks. I never questioned his answer as I thought the waterworks was the drinking water for Chagford. A couple of years later when he brought up some more tomatoes I started to wonder.

I was sitting on a pile of tyres when he walked down the path towards my Father, carrying a box of tomatoes. It was then I remembered what he'd told me a few years before. I couldn't understand how tomatoes could grow in water every year.

Handing the box to Father he turned to say 'Hello' as he walked past to look around the yard, so I asked him. In a matter-of-fact tone he said, 'When you eat tomatoes the seed goes straight through you, down the toilet, then down into the waterworks.' All I could do was shriek 'Yuk! You give us tomatoes out of shit!' He started laughing and a smile spread across his face. 'You don't eat the seed, just the tomatoes off the plant.' 'Yuk!' I replied.

I never ate his tomatoes from that day on. Even now when I get given tomatoes I just hope they have been grown in a growbag.

Cider Vinegar

Arthur Routley was out visiting the scrapyard one day. Sam was out picking up scrap so Mother invited Arthur in for a cup of tea while he waited. She asked Arthur how he was keeping. He said that he hadn't been well: his kidney stones were causing him a lot of pain. Mother told Arthur that she could cure them, using herbs. She'd helped many people in the past. Arthur didn't fancy going to hospital for treatment and was willing to try anything; he'd already had a hospital consultation and had been put off by the personal nature of the procedure (there was only one way in – and it wasn't by knife!). Mother told him all he had to do was buy a bottle of pure cider vinegar and take it first thing in the morning before breakfast for about six weeks (or until he couldn't stomach it any more).

Mother explained, 'If you don't think it'll work go home and put an eggshell in a glass, cover it in cider vinegar and watch it dissolve. It's only calcium, and that's what kidney stones are.'

Arthur went home and took the cider vinegar for as long as he could put up with it, and within six weeks he had passed them. They were as long as rat shit. His doctor called him in, and told Arthur that they were going to have to do something about his kidney stones. Arthur told his doctor that there wasn't any need as he had already passed them and had kept them in a jam jar to prove it. To this day he keeps them in a jam jar in the cupboard.

Sam with Clare, Peggy's daughter, 1986 *Courtesy of Peggy Harris*

IN CONCLUSION

After Sam died in 1988, the scrapyard continued for another ten years. However, new rules and regulations, coupled with a dramatic drop in the value of scrap, eventually forced its closure. Bob Harris stills lives at Lettaford, but works as a mechanic in Bovey Tracey. The rest of the family eventually moved into Exeter and live separately. Peggy says of city life: 'My house is just four walls really, somewhere to rest my head. I miss Dartmoor, the stillness, the river, listening to the foxes barking up through the valley and if I could afford to move back home I would. But there's no work for me on Dartmoor now, and it's all got too expensive.

ACKNOWLEDGEMENTS

None of this would have been possible without Chris Chapman. I'd shown my stories to several people before taking them to Chris, and he was the first person to take me (and them) seriously. He set the ball rolling by getting some of the stories published in *Dartmoor Magazine*, and he's made me feel I've achieved something in my life. I don't think he realises quite how much this means to me.

I would also like to thank my daughter Clare for typing up the stories, and for putting up with me! And thank you to everyone else who has helped me along the way.